FUMBLE-FREE:
A FOOTBALL COOKBOOK

FUMBLE-FREE:
A FOOTBALL COOKBOOK

by LORRAINE SHEFFIELD

Eagle Shore Press   Anchorage, Alaska

To my parents, Bobbie and Doyle Barnett

Copyright © 1991 by Lorraine Sheffield

All rights reserved. No part of this book may be reproduced or utilized in any form or by any means, electronic or mechanical, including photocopying, recording or by any information storage and retrieval system, without written permission from the publishser.

This book is a celebration of football. References in it to players, teams and stadiums are not intended and should not be construed to imply any sponsorship or endorsement by or other association with any such individuals, teams, organizations or companies.

Published by: Eagle Shore Press
P.O. Box 92377
Anchorage, Alaska 99509-2477

First Printing November, 1991.
Printed in U.S.A.

Library of Congress Catalog Card Number: 91-093134

ISBN 0-9631021-6-8

Book Design and Illustrations by:
Art & International Productions
Jim Tilly & Sasha Sagan

Cover Illustration, Design and Photography:
Sasha Sagan

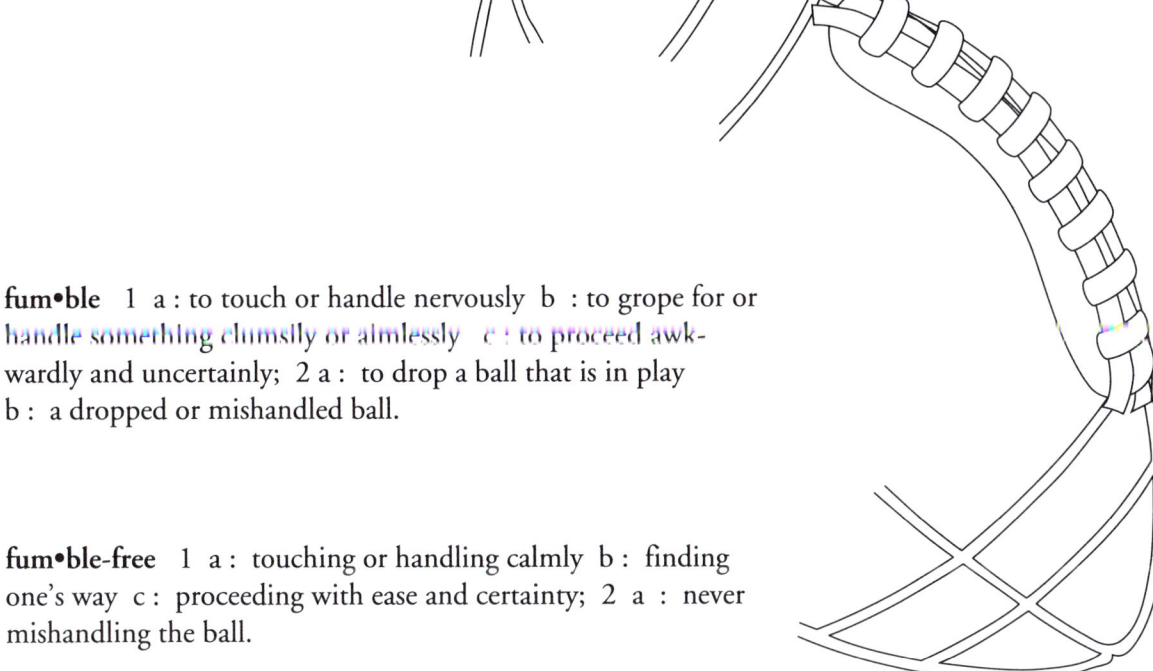

fum•ble 1 a : to touch or handle nervously b : to grope for or handle something clumsily or aimlessly c : to proceed awkwardly and uncertainly; 2 a : to drop a ball that is in play b : a dropped or mishandled ball.

fum•ble-free 1 a : touching or handling calmly b : finding one's way c : proceeding with ease and certainty; 2 a : never mishandling the ball.

FUM•BLE-FREE: A FOOT•BALL COOK•BOOK
1 a : a book of recipes you can use when someone asks "What dish would you like to bring?" b : handling football parties or casual entertaining calmly c : having over 185 recipes that are easy to prepare, economical and applause-winning; 2 a : to learn the basics of football to better enjoy the game b : expansion of your knowledge of football in a way that is fun, easy and simple 3 a : in football or cooking—never dropping the ball.

TABLE OF CONTENTS

INTRODUCTION	9
HOW TO ORGANIZE A SUCCESSFUL FOOTBALL PARTY	10
THE KICKOFF—APPETIZERS	16
BOWLS AND STADIUMS—SALADS	48
FOOTBALL FIELD & POSITIONS	76
OFFENSE AND DEFENSE—ENTREES	78
TERMS AND RULES—BREADS	107
SUDDEN DEATH—DESSERTS	123
FIELD SUPPORT—SPECIAL DISHES	155
MENUS	164
FUSSY FANS—CHILDREN'S FOOD	170
SUPER BOWL—PARTY FARE	173
DRESSING ROOM—DRESSINGS	190
ROOKIE RECIPE TIPS—BASICS	192
WINNERS—ACKNOWLEDGMENTS	195
GUESS THE SCORE	196
BIBLIOGRAPHY	198
INDEX	199

INTRODUCTION

I'm a football nut. Ever since viewing the 1958 championship game between the Baltimore Colts and the New York Giants I've been a football fan. The Colts, quarterbacked by Johnny Unitas won in sudden-death overtime. Dad and I spent every Sunday that season perched before our television set. I was as unfamiliar with football as I was with my quiet, hard-working father. Today, thanks to Dad I know football. More importantly, thanks to football I know Dad.

Over the years I've tried to combine two passions—cooking and football. Sunday afternoons my television sits on a kitchen counter tuned to NFL games. The pots on the stove are tuned to turning out meals for the busy week ahead or just experimenting with new recipes. Noticeable cooking fumbles sometimes occur when I pay more attention to a spectacular maneuver by a running back and forget an important ingredient. I've missed some key plays, too, while engrossed in a culinary project.

Over the years I've learned not everyone shares my interest in sports. I wrote this book to convey a simple understanding of football. It's intended as a basic primer of terms, rules, information and some of the game's heroes.

The dishes are just the same—basic, easy, intended to score points with your guests. There are over 185 recipes, suggested game menus, ideas for organizing football parties, tips on meal preparation or ingredients and ideas for your Super Bowl fare. After trying some of these dishes you should know a little more about football. You may never be a football nut, but you may be a food hero, enjoying the applause of your dining crowd whenever you serve Tight End Chiladas, Linebacker Basil Burgers or Roughing the Kicker Kabobs.

This book is a celebration of football—the game, the players and more. It's also fumble-free.

HOW TO ORGANIZE A SUCCESSFUL FOOTBALL PARTY

1. ***The Draft***—contact friends, couples, singles and/or co-workers, (from here on, referred to as fans) to gather for a football party.
    - 6-18 fans works best.

2. ***The First Party***:
    - Host the initial football party in your home.
    - Let the fans know what you will prepare for an entree.
    - Have each fan (couple or single) bring one of the following:

appetizer	salad
bread	support dishes for entree

    - For large groups additional appetizers or beverages may be included.

3. ***Season Kickoff***:
    - If you wish to gather on a regular basis, eg. Monday nights, provide a calendar of all Mondays from September through the first two weeks of December. Some newspapers publish a schedule of NFL games. (They will list the teams playing each Monday night as well as weekend games.)

    - Have fans sign up to host one or more football parties.

    - Obtain addresses and phone numbers of the group members.

    - Designate one person as the Football Party Commissioner. The commissioner is in charge of scheduling and distribution of phone lists.

    - Decide the following:
        - Will there be some type of betting on the quarter score? (Instructions and a grid sample are provided under **GUESS THE SCORE**)
        - If the home team will provide any or all beverages?

4. Helpful hints:

- Eliminate phone calls. Decide during fourth quarter every week what food selection each fan will prepare the following week using dishes from FUMBLE-FREE: A FOOTBALL COOKBOOK.

- Some dishes may need baking or reheating upon arrival. Check ahead with the home team. Coordinate oven use.

5. Responsibilities for the "Home Team":

- Prepare entree.

- Set up buffet area with silverware, napkins, plates and condiments.

- Set out grid sheet and container for money if you're playing Guess the Score, page 196.

- Have sufficient ice available for drinks.

- Provide soft drinks, wine, or beer if fans have selected that option.

6. Extras:

- Your FUMBLE-FREE: A FOOTBALL COOKBOOK contains football facts and trivia. Print a few of these items on cards. Place cards around the buffet and coffee tables.

- Color-coordinate your accessories—i.e. paper napkins—with the colors of the two teams. (See page 199)

OFFICIAL RULES

TIMING

(Or why does a game last over 3 hours?)

There are four quarters in a professional football game.
- *Each quarter is 15 minutes
- *Intermission between the periods is 2 minutes
- *Halftime is 12 minutes (unless otherwise specified).
- *Teams change goals after each quarter.
- *Ties may be decided by one or more 15 minute sudden death overtimes.

Timeouts occur during a game and the clock is stopped for the following: (not including television's needs)
- *Each team is allowed three 1-1/2 minute time outs each half.
- *Referees can allow timeouts for:
    - Player injury, 2 minutes
    - Equipment repair, 3 minutes
- *Automatic time-outs occur:
    - Following a score—touchdown or field goal
    - Following a change of possession
    - During a try-for-point attempt
    - At the end of a down when a foul occurs

OFFICIAL RULES

FUMBLE-FREE: A FOOTBALL COOKBOOK

-------TERMS------

<u>HOME TEAM:</u>   Team that hosts the fans and prepares the entree.

<u>FANS:</u> Guests who arrive with any of the following:
an appetizer, bread, salad, dessert or other dish or beverages.

<u>PRE-GAME:</u> Food preparation at home.

-------TIMING-------
*Use "Official Rules—Timing"
to gauge preparation and presentation.

<u>FIRST QUARTER:</u> Set out appetizers

- Some dishes may need baking or reheating. Check ahead regarding oven use.
- Use the "*Two-Minute Warning*" before the *Half* for some of the following activities:
    Tossing the salad and dressing
    Slicing bread
    Setting up or slicing the entree or dessert

<u>HALF-TIME:</u> Set out the salad, entree, bread and any other dish that may accompany the entree.

<u>THIRD QUARTER:</u> Dessert may be served now or during the *Fourth Quarter.*

STARTING PLAY

...and the home of the brave!" For a brief moment the last note is held suspended. The anticipation of players, coaches and fans suddenly ignites the chill night air. As if by magic the referee's whistle transforms America for the next 5 months. Monday nights and weekends are dictated by those who worship football before their television screens. From livingrooms to sport's bars football and technology capture our lives and hold our culture hostage.

THE KICKOFF

Appetizers begin your football party just as **THE KICKOFF** begins the game.

THE BALL

The ball, or "pigskin," is oval-shaped and covered with a pebbled grain leather. Steerhide, not pigskin, is the preferred material. Cowhide is second choice.
- Length: 11-1/2 inches
- Circumference: 28-1/2 inches at widest part
- Weight: 14-15 ounces

The home team must have 24 footballs available for testing one hour before the game.

PEPPERED CHEESE BALL

- 2 cups (8 ounces) Monterey Jack cheese, grated
- 1 (8-ounce) package cream cheese, softened
- 1 teaspoon fines herbes
- 1 teaspoon minced chives
- 1 teaspoon Worcestershire sauce
- 1 garlic clove, crushed
- 2-3 tablespoons seasoned pepper
- Plain or bacon-flavored crackers

PRE-GAME:
In bowl, combine Jack cheese, cream cheese, fines herbes, chives, Worcestershire sauce and garlic.
Shape cheese mixture into 5" ball; slightly flatten one side.
On a square of waxed paper spread seasoned pepper in an even thick layer.
Roll cheese ball in pepper until completely covered.
Refrigerate 6 hours or overnight. Cheese ball can be stored in refrigerator several days before serving.

FIRST QUARTER:
Serve with crackers or pear slices.

OLIVE CHEESE BALL

- 2 (8-ounce) packages cream cheese
- 1 (14-ounce) package blue cheese or crumbled blue cheese
- 1/4 cup soft margarine
- 1 small can sliced ripe olives
- 2 tablespoons minced onion
- 3 drops Tabasco sauce
- Garlic salt to taste
- Worcestershire sauce (optional)
- Pecans, chopped
- Parsley, minced
- Paprika

PRE-GAME:
Mix together first 8 ingredients and chill. Shape into a ball. Roll in nuts, parsley or paprika.

FIRST QUARTER: Serve with melba rounds.

PARMESAN CHEESE BALL

- 1 (8-ounce) package cream cheese
- 1/2 cup Parmesan cheese
- 1/4 teaspoon garlic
- 1/4 cup pimiento
- 1/4 cup chopped green pepper
- Parsley (optional)

PRE-GAME:
Mix ingredients; chill and shape into football.
Use chives to simulate stictching on top)or roll in minced parsley).

FIRST QUARTER: Serve with crackers.

SALMON BALL

- 1 (1-pound) can red (sockeye) salmon
- 1 (8-ounce) package cream cheese, softened
- 1 tablespoon lemon juice
- 2 teaspoons onion, minced
- 1 teaspoon horseradish
- 1/4 teaspoon salt
- 1/2 teaspoon liquid smoke
- 1/2 cup pecans, chopped
- 3 tablespoons parsley, finely chopped

PRE-GAME:
Drain salmon, remove bones, skin; break apart salmon pieces. Mix all other ingredients with salmon except pecans and parsley. Chill at least 4 hours or overnight. Mix parsley and nuts. Roll ball in this mixture. Chill.

FIRST QUARTER: Serve with a variety of crackers.

THE FIELD

The playing field is 120 yards long and 53-1/2 yards wide. People often think it's 100 yards long. They forget to include the end zone—10 yards at each end of the field. Goal lines are considered within the end zones. Lines running perpendicular to the 5-yard and 10-yard markers are the side lines. Players in possession of the ball will be declared out-of-bounds if they go beyond the side lines.

Hashmarks appear on the field and are 70 feet, 9 inches from each sideline.

Goal posts must be painted bright gold. They are placed at both ends of the field offset from the end line. Their crossbars are within the plane of each goal line. The posts measure 10 feet above the ground. The crossbar is 18 feet, 6 inches in length. Uprights, perpendicular to the crossbar, are 20 feet high. The actual plane of each goal extends indefinitely above the crossbar—beyond the outer edges of the posts.

VEGETABLE SQUARES

- 2 bunches green onions, finely sliced
- 2 tablespoons margarine
- 1 (10-ounce) package frozen chopped spinach, thawed, drained
- 1/4 cup parsley, minced
- 1/2 teaspoon salt
- 1/8 teaspoon freshly ground pepper
- 6 eggs
- 1/4 cup sour cream
- 1/2 cup seasoned bread crumbs
- 3/4 cup (3 ounces) natural Swiss cheese, grated
- 3/4 cup grated Parmesan cheese
- Paprika

PRE-GAME:

Saute onions in margarine until limp. Drain spinach well (press between paper towels after draining); finely chop spinach and add to onions. Cook 1 minute. Remove from heat; add parsley, salt and pepper.

In a bowl, beat eggs; stir in sour cream, bread crumbs, Swiss cheese and 1/2 cup Parmesan. Blend well. Stir into spinach-onion mixture.

Pour into greased 9" square baking pan. Sprinkle remaining Parmesan cheese and dust with paprika for color. Bake at 350 degrees for 20 minutes or until a knife inserted comes out clean.

Cool slightly. Cut into squares.

FIRST QUARTER:

Reheat slightly or serve at room temperature.

Note: Recipe may also double as a vegetable dish with an entree.

EGGPLANT APPETIZER

1 large eggplant
1 medium onion, chopped
1/2 bell pepper, chopped
2 tablespoons olive oil
2 tablespoons margarine
1 large tomato, peeled and chopped
2 tablespoons lemon juice
1 tablespoon ketchup
1/2 teaspoon Worcestershire sauce
1/4 teaspoon salt
Dill weed
Chives, chopped
Parsley, chopped
Sliced black olives

WHOLE WHEAT PITA CRISPS

1 package (6-inch) whole wheat pita bread
1/2 cup butter
Garlic powder and parsley
Dried oregano leaves
Dried tarragon
Dried dill
1 cup finely grated Romano cheese

PRE-GAME:
Bake eggplant in greased pan at 400 degrees for 20 minutes. Remove and cool. Peel and chop.
Saute onion and bell pepper in oil until tender, not brown.
Add margarine, tomato, lemon juice, ketchup, Worcestershire, salt and dill weed. Cook over high heat, stirring until liquid has evaporated. Refrigerate until an hour before serving.

PITA BREAD CRISPS:
Cut around edge of pita bread and butter both halves; sprinkle with garlic powder.
Separate halves into 2 or more groups and top with your favorite herbs.
Dill and oregano are excellent.
You may wish to try tarragon, green onion, chive, etc.
Sprinkle each pita with Romano cheese. Broil until golden brown.
Cut pitas into fourths.

FIRST QUARTER:
Serve eggplant appetizer at room temperature.
Sprinkle with chives, parsley and olives.
Serve with pita bread crisps.

MARINATED MUSHROOMS

1 pound small whole mushroom caps

MARINADE

3/4 cup salad oil
3/4 cup red wine vinegar
1/4 cup onion, finely chopped
1/4 cup parsley, finely chopped
2 cloves garlic, crushed
1 teaspoon salt
1 teaspoon sugar

PRE-GAME:
Wash mushrooms thoroughly; allow to dry.
MARINADE: Mix all ingredients.
Marinate mushrooms in refrigerator four or more hours.
(Overnight is even better.)

FIRST QUARTER:
Arrange mushrooms on a bed of lettuce.

Mushrooms
Button mushrooms should have smooth caps that are closed around their stems. Store in refrigerator in paper towels. When ready to use, wash carefully removing dirt particles. Allow to dry at least 30 minutes on a paper towel.

STUFFED MUSHROOMS

1/2 cup butter or margarine
6 tablespoons Jack cheese
4 tablespoons red wine
2 teaspoons soy sauce
2/3 cup cracker crumbs
2 garlic cloves, crushed
1 pound small whole mushrooms, stems removed

PRE-GAME:
Mix ingredients and stuff into mushrooms.

FIRST QUARTER:
Broil 5" from heat for 3 minutes until bubbly; serve.

SCRIMMAGE SPINACH

2 cups sour cream
1 pinch garlic powder
1 cup mayonnaise
3/4 package dry leek soup mix
1 (10-ounce) package frozen chopped spinach, drained, re-chop
1/2 cup fresh parsley, finely chopped
1/2 cup green onions, finely chopped
1 teaspoon dill weed
1 teaspoon salad seasoning
1 (5-ounce) can sliced water chestnuts
1 loaf round crusty bread
Optional: 1 loaf crusty bread for bread cubes

PRE-GAME:
Combine sour cream, garlic powder and mayonnaise. Add soup mix; blend thoroughly. Add spinach, parsley, green onions, dill, salad seasoning and water chestnuts; mix. Cut circle in top of one loaf of bread; hollow out. Slice other loaf into cubes.

FIRST QUARTER:
Place dip into the hollowed-out bread and serve with bread cubes and/or an assortment of raw vegetables—carrots, celery, green pepper, cauliflower, broccoli, and zucchini.

ARTICHOKE NIBBLES

2 jars artichoke hearts
1 small onion, chopped
1 clove garlic, minced
4 eggs, beaten
1/4 cup bread crumbs
1/4 teaspoon salt
1/8 teaspoon pepper
1/8 teaspoon oregano
1/8 teaspoon Tabasco sauce
1/2 cup Parmesan cheese
1/2 pound sharp cheddar cheese, grated

PRE-GAME:
Drain 1 jar artichoke hearts and place liquid in skillet. Drain other jar and discard liquid. Chop artichoke hearts. Set aside. Cook onion and garlic in skillet with liquid. Combine ingredients. Press into greased 8" pan. Bake at 325 degrees for 30 minutes.

FIRST QUARTER:
Reheat nibbles at 325 degrees for 10 minutes.

LINE OF SCRIMMAGE
The line of scrimmage for each team is a line passing through the end of the ball closest to and parallel to the team's own goal line. The area between the two lines of scrimmage is the neutral zone.

THE COIN TOSS

The coin toss occurs in the center of the field two minutes before kickoff. The visiting captain calls "heads" or "tails." The winner of the toss has two choices:

1) Receive or kick the ball
2) Which goal his team will defend

The loser of the toss receives the other choice. However, prior to kickoff of the second half, the loser receives first choice of the above.

If team arrives late onto the field prior to scheduled kickoff, they may be penalized 15 yards and loss of coin toss option.

CAVIAR MOUSSE

- 1 envelope unflavored gelatin
- 1/4 cup cold water
- 1 (8-ounce) package cream cheese, softened
- 1/2 cup plain yogurt
- 2 tablespoons fresh parsley, chopped
- 1 tablespoon lemon juice
- 1/4 teaspoon pepper
- 2 teaspoons green onion, sliced
- 1 (2-ounce) jar black caviar
- 1 (2-ounce) jar red salmon caviar
- 3/4 cup whipping cream

PRE-GAME:
Soften gelatin in small bowl over cold water for 5 minutes.
Mix cream cheese, yogurt, parsley, lemon juice, onion and pepper.
Place bowl of gelatin over boiling water and stir to dissolve.
When dissolved, stir into cheese mixture.
Refrigerate for 15 minutes to thicken.
Drain black and red caviar separately.
Handle gently to avoid breaking any beads.
Rinse with cold water. Pat dry with paper towels.
Divide mixture into two separate bowls.
Fold black caviar into one bowl and the red caviar into another.
Lightly oil a 4-cup ring mold.
Spoon red caviar mixture into the mold and freeze for 5-8 minutes.
Spoon black caviar mixture atop the red caviar.
Cover and chill 3 or hours more.

FIRST QUARTER:
Unmold and serve with cucumber slices and crackers.

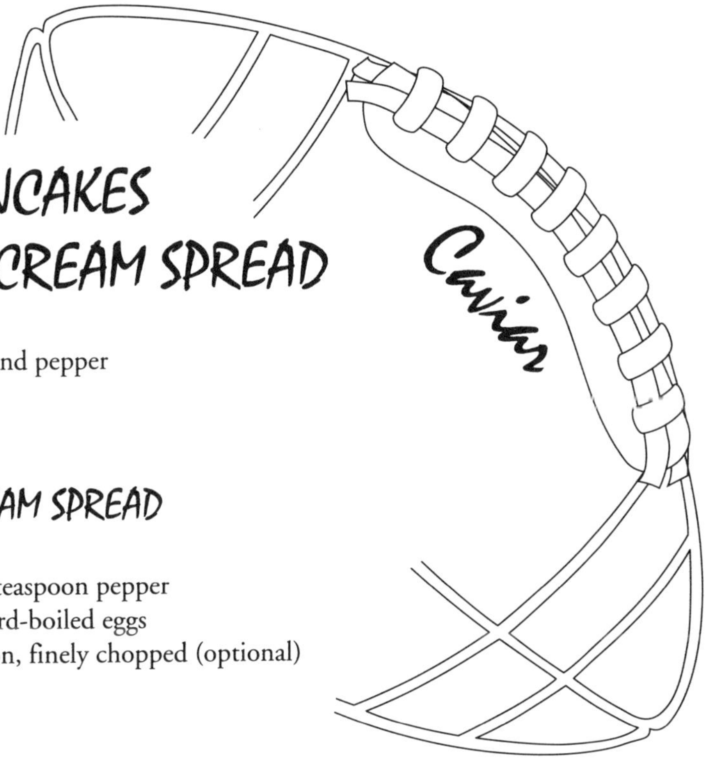

POTATO PANCAKES WITH CAVIAR SOUR CREAM SPREAD

4 large russet potatoes
2 tablespoons flour
1 egg, beaten
Salt and pepper
Oil

CAVIAR SOUR CREAM SPREAD

1/2 cup sour cream
1 (4-ounce) jar black caviar
1 teaspoon grated onion
2 teaspoons lemon juice
1/8 teaspoon pepper
3 hard-boiled eggs
Onion, finely chopped (optional)

PRE-GAME:
Peel and shred potatoes; press out excess water.
Mix with flour, egg and seasonings.
Form into patties and fry in oil. Oil should just coat the pan to keep the pancakes from sticking. Dry on paper towels.

SOUR CREAM SPREAD:
Combine sour cream, caviar, onion, lemon juice and pepper. Chill.
Sieve hard-boiled eggs.

FIRST QUARTER:
Reheat pancakes a few minutes in 400-degree oven.
Serve with Caviar Sour Cream Spread. Garnish spread with eggs and onion.

Note: It's a toss up whether or not your fans enjoy caviar.

THE SNAP

The snap occurs at the line of scrimmage. Technically, it is a backward pass through the legs of the center. Some of the rules for the snap are:

1) The offensive team must have 7 players on the line of scrimmage.
2) All players, except the player receiving the snap, must be at least one yard behind the line of scrimmage.
3) No interior lineman may move after taking or simulating a three-point stance.
4) No player of the offensive team may charge or move, after assuming set position, in such a manner as to lead the defense to believe the snap has started.
5) All players of the offensive team must be stationary at the snap, except one back who may be in motion parallel to the scrimmage line or backward (not forward).
6) After a shift or huddle all players on the offensive team must come to an absolute stop for at least one second with no movement of the hands, feet, head, or (swaying of the) body.
7) Quarterbacks can be called for a false start penalty (5 yards) if their actions are judged to be an obvious attempt to draw an opponent offside.

CHILI CON QUESO

1 large can tomatoes
1 large onion, chopped fine
1-1/2 pounds American cheese
1/2 pound cheddar cheese
1 (7-ounce) can chopped green chiles
1 clove garlic, chopped
3-4 stalks celery, chopped

PRE-GAME:
Drain tomatoes and place in double boiler. Add chopped onion and cook 10 minutes. Cut cheese into cubes, add to tomatoes and stir until dissolved. Add remaining ingredients.

FIRST QUARTER:
Serve with hunks of warm French bread, crackers or a variety of tortilla chips.

TEX MEX BEEF DIP

2 (12-ounce) cans roast beef *
1 (7-ounce) can diced green chiles
1/2 pound longhorn cheese, cubed
1/2 pound cheddar cheese, cubed
1 (10-to-19 ounce) can stewed tomatoes
2 green onions, chopped
1 (4-ounce) can chopped black olives
Salt and pepper.

PRE-GAME:
Heat beef and break apart.
*Try this as an alternative to canned meat: select a 3 to 3-1/2 pound pot roast. Place in a Dutch oven or large pot and fill with enough water to cover half the meat. Bake at 350 degrees for several hours until roast is moist and stringy. Use half or more of the meat for this recipe. Save the rest for sandwiches.
Add remaining ingredients. Cook over low heat 15 minutes. (Pour most of the liquid away.)

FIRST QUARTER:
Serve appetizer warm with a variety of tortilla chips, slices of French bread or stuffed into potato skins.
(See Sombrero filling for skins' preparation.)

Note: Take any leftovers home and use in flour tortillas for another meal.

TURNOVER
Play in which other team ends up with the ball—usually by a fumble or interception.

TORTILLA TURNOVERS

6 (8-inch) flour tortillas
1 (12-ounce) package whipped cream cheese
1/3 cup cheddar cheese, grated
3 tablespoons green chiles
3 tablespoons chopped ripe olives
1 small jar chopped pimiento
4 green onions, minced
Dash garlic powder

PRE-GAME:
Combine all ingredients. Spread mixture completely over each tortilla. Turnover or roll each tortilla—jelly-roll style. Wrap with plastic wrap. Refrigerate several hours.
Slice each roll into half-inch rounds.

LAYERED MEXICAN DIP

4 avocados
4 teaspoons grated onion
Juice of 2 lemons
Salt and pepper
1-1/2 cups sour cream
1/2 cup mayonnaise
1 (16-ounce) can spicy refried beans
1 cup salsa
1 bunch green onions
2 (3-1/2 ounce) cans chopped black olives
3/4 pound sharp cheddar cheese, grated
1/2 pound ground beef
1 small onion, chopped
1 package Taco seasoning
1 (7-ounce) can diced green chiles

TOPPING

3 tomatoes, chopped
2 green onions
2 tablespoons cilantro, chopped
Salt and pepper

PRE-GAME:

Mash avocados with onion, lemon juice, salt and pepper. Mix sour cream with mayonnaise. Layer the following in a 9-1/2" x 11" dish or pan: refried beans, avocado mixture, sour cream and mayonnaise mixture, salsa, green onions, black olives and cheddar cheese.
Seal with plastic wrap and refrigerate.
Saute ground beef and onions. Drain. Toss with taco seasoning and diced green chiles. Refrigerate.

FIRST QUARTER:

Reheat meat mixture slightly. Layer meat mixture on cheddar cheese. Top with tomatoes, green onions and cilantro.

PILING ON
Charging into the ball carrier or any player on the ground intentionally may be ruled as piling on. The offending team is awarded a 15-yard penalty.

TAXI-SQUAD TORTILLA PIE

5 small flour tortillas
2 tablespoons margarine
1/2 cup onion, thinly sliced
1/2 cup green pepper, thinly sliced
1/2 cup fresh mushrooms, sliced
1 teaspoon salt
1 small can chopped green chiles (optional)
3 eggs
1-1/2 tablespoons sugar
3 tablespoons flour
1/2 teaspoon baking powder
1/2 cup milk
1/2 cup cheddar cheese, shredded
1/2 cup Jack cheese, shredded
1 avocado, peeled and thinly sliced
1 tomato, sliced
4 ounces cheddar cheese, shredded

PRE-GAME:
Spray large pie pan with non-stick oil. Lay tortillas around the dish leaving 2" of tortilla extending over the top.
Saute onion, green pepper and mushrooms in margarine. Sprinkle with salt. When cool, add chiles and pour mixture over tortillas. In mixing bowl, beat eggs and sugar. Add flour and baking powder alternating with the milk. Fold in cheese. Place egg mixture on top onion mixture.
Arrange avocado and tomato slices over all.
Fold over tortillas and keep in place with wooden toothpicks.
Place remaining 4 oz. cheese over opening in center.
Bake at 350 degrees, 40-45 minutes.

FIRST QUARTER:
Slice pie in wedges. Cover with foil and reheat in 300-degree oven until warm. Allow 10 minutes to set before serving.

GUACAMOLE DUNK

2 ripe avocados
1 tablespoon fresh lime juice
6 tablespoons mayonnaise
2 tablespoons freshly grated onion
    and its juice
Garlic salt
Freshly ground pepper
Cayenne pepper, pinch
1 teaspoon chili powder
Dash of Tabasco sauce
3 slices bacon, cooked
    and crumbled (optional)

PRE-GAME:
Peel and pit avocados, then dice. Sprinkle with lime juice.
Place in blender and add remaining ingredients. Place in bowl. Add bacon.

FIRST QUARTER:
Serve with a variety of tortilla chips.

TAXI SQUAD
In the late 1940's Art McBride owned not only the Cleveland Browns, but a taxicab company too. A 33-man playing roster was required in those days. McBride would give jobs as cabbies to the cut players. To replace players he turned to his stable of taxi drivers.

Today there's a reserve list for players not immediately available to play (injury, military service, etc.). They may not practice or return to the Active List until four regular season games have been played.

ON THE NUMBERS NACHOS

1/2 pound ground beef
1/2 pound chorizo sausage (remove casing)
1 or 2 (1 pound each) cans refried beans
1 (7-ounce) can chopped green chiles
2-3 cups mild cheddar cheese, shredded
3/4 cup prepared taco sauce

6 green onions, sliced
1 cup sliced ripe olives
1 cup thawed avocado dip
1 medium ripe avocado
1 cup sour cream

PRE-GAME:
Brown beef and chorizo sausage, drain. Season beef with salt if needed. Place in baking/serving dish. Spread refried beans on top of meat. Sprinkle chiles over beans. Top with cheddar cheese. Spread taco sauce over cheese. Bake uncovered at 400 degrees 20-25 minutes.

FIRST QUARTER:
Reheat at 400 degrees 5-10 minutes.
Top with green onions, ripe olives, avocado dip, avocados and sour cream.
Serve with a variety of tortilla chips
(nacho-flavored, ranch, blue corn etc).

The following jersey numbering system is used in the NFL.
1-19
Quarterbacks & specialists
20-49
Running backs & defensive backs
50-59
Centers & linebackers
60-79
Defensive linemen and interior offensive linemen (other than centers)
80-89
Wide receivers, tight ends and flanker backs.

HEARTY QUESADILLAS

8 corn or flour tortillas
1/4 cup salsa
2 cups Monterey Jack cheese, grated
1 cup green onions, thinly sliced

2 cups cooked chicken or turkey, shredded
1 can whole kernel corn, drained
Guacamole
Sour cream

PRE-GAME:
Place 4 tortillas on cookie sheet.
On each tortilla spread: 1 tablespoons salsa, 1/4 cup Jack cheese
  1/4 cup onions, 1/2 cup chicken or turkey,
  2 tablespoons whole kernel corn and 1/4 cup Jack cheese.
Place tortilla on top of each, pressing lightly. Refrigerate.

FIRST QUARTER:
Bake at 375 degrees 9-12 minutes or until cheese melts. Cut into wedges. Serve with guacamole, sour cream and/or salsa.

Yield: 16 wedges

MEXICALI SOMBRERO SKINS

1 pound ground round
1/2 onion, chopped
2 (8-ounce) cans kidney beans, mashed
1-1/2 cups cheddar cheese, grated
1/2 cup ketchup
1 teaspoon chili powder
1-2 drops Tabasco sauce

PRE-GAME:
Saute onion; add ground round, brown lightly. Drain mixture.
Mix all ingredients in bowl.
Fill prepared potato skins with meat mixture.
Bake at 350 degrees 10-15 minutes, or until warm.

FIRST QUARTER:
Reheat potato skins. Top with sliced black olives and green onions. Serve with sour cream, guacamole or ranch dressing.

POTATO SKINS

Bag of very small russet potatoes

PRE-GAME:
Wash skins. Rub skins with a little olive oil and prick with fork or sharp knife.
(*Optional:* sprinkle with seasoning salt and seasoned pepper.)
Bake potatoes at 400 degrees until done.
Cool skins. When cool enough to handle, slice in half and scoop out contents leaving an edge of potato 1/4" thick around the skin.
May be returned to oven and baked 20 minutes. Fill skins.
May be frozen unfilled. Keep in plastic bags.

Other combinations with potato skins:
Bacon-Cheese: Combine bacon (cooked and crumbled), cheddar cheese, green onions, sour cream, salt and pepper. Cook until cheese has melted.

Chicken Oriental: Combine cooked chicken, onion (cooked until limp), teriyaki sauce and garlic salt. Heat in oven. Remove. Sprinkle with sesame seeds.

Spicy Pizza: Combine browned Italian sausage and onions with pizza sauce, oregano and garlic salt. Top with mozzarella cheese. Cook until cheese has melted.

GREAT FOOTBALL COMBINATIONS
<u>San Diego</u>
Dan Fouts and Chuck Muncie
<u>Miami</u>
Larry Czonka "Mr. Inside," Mercury Morris "Mr. Outside" and Jim Klick.
<u>San Franscisco</u>
Joe Montana and Jerry Rice
<u>Dallas</u>
Roger Staubach and Drew Pearson. Don Meredith and Bob Hayes
<u>Pittsburgh</u>
Terry Bradshaw and Lynn Swann

THE DOWN

The down begins when the ball is put into play and ends when the ball is dead. A team has four downs to advance the ball 10 yards. Any time a team earns 10 yards they receive a first down. This entitles them to another sequence of four downs.

Often the "chain crew" will be motioned onto the field. If any part of the ball is advanced 10 yards, the offensive team earns a first down.

PIMIENTO DIP

- 2 eggs, beaten
- 1/4 cup vinegar
- 2 tablespoons sugar
- 1 (8-ounce) package cream cheese
- 1 medium onion, chopped
- 1 green pepper, chopped
- 1 small jar pimientos chopped

PRE-GAME:
Cook eggs with vinegar and sugar until thick, stirring constantly. Pour over cream cheese and whip until mixture is smooth.
Add remaining ingredients.
Refrigerate overnight.

FIRST QUARTER:
Serve with a variety of potato chips or crackers.

REUBEN DIP

- 1 (8-ounce) package cream cheese, softened
- 1/2 cup sour cream
- 1 cup shredded Swiss cheese
- 8 ounces sliced corned beef, finely diced
- 1/2 cup drained sauerkraut, chopped
- 4-6 tablespoons milk

PRE-GAME:
Heat ingredients in saucepan over low heat. Thin with milk if necessary.

FIRST QUARTER:
Serve warm with rye sticks or rye rounds.

HOT CRAB DIP

- 1 (7-ounce) can crabmeat
- 1 (8-ounce) package cream cheese, softened
- 1 teaspoon Worcestershire sauce
- 2 drops Tabasco
- 1-1/2 teaspoons seasoning salt
- 1 teaspoon lemon juice
- 1/2 medium onion, finely chopped
- 1/2 cup cheddar cheese, grated

PRE-GAME:
Mix ingredients except cheddar cheese.
Top with grated cheese.
Bake at 325 degrees for 20 minutes.

FIRST QUARTER:
Reheat for a few minutes or place in an electric fondue pot or chafing dish. Be careful mixture doesn't burn.
Serve with wheat thins or French bread cubes.

NASTURTIUM DIP

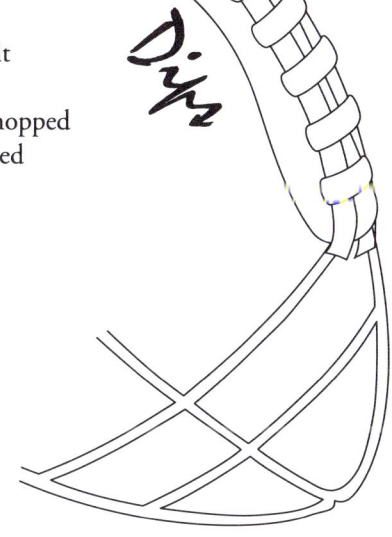

NASTY
Code name for the wide receiver when he is lined up 3-5 yards from the offensive tackle.

- 1 bunch radishes
- 4 green onions, sliced
- 1 teaspoon lemon juice
- 1 (8-ounce) package cream cheese, softened.
- 1/4 cup celery, thinly sliced
- 1 tablespoon nasturtium leaves
- Celery and cucumbers
- Nasturtium petals

PRE-GAME:
Shred radishes in food processor. Mix with remaining ingredients.
Stuff celery and/or serve atop cucumber slices.
Garnish with petals.

Edible Flowers:
Nasturtium leaves have a pleasant peppery taste. Some pesticide-free leaves and petals of other flowers can be used in many dishes. Make sure they are organically grown. Check with your local poison control center or state extension service if you're unsure what to use. Try pansies, bachelor's button, apple or chive blossoms, roses and calendulas for a beautiful rice salad presentation.

AVOCADO CRAB DIP

3 or 4 medium avocados
1 teaspoon grated onion
1/2 teaspoon seasoned salt
1/2 teaspoon garlic salt
1 tablespoon lemon juice
1/2 cup sour cream
1 teaspoon horseradish
2 (7-3/4-ounce) cans crabmeat, drained and flaked or imitation crab
2 drops hot pepper sauce (optional)

PRE-GAME:
Cut avocados in half, remove pit and peel; mash pulp or blend in food processor. Add remaining ingredients and mix well.

FIRST QUARTER:
Serve with tortilla chips or crackers.

AVOCADOS

To ripen an avocado quickly, store in flour canister for a day—twenty-four hours later a soft, ripe avocado awaits.

Easiest method to peel avocado: Cut in half lengthwise and separate the two halves. Cradle avocado half with pit in palm of your hand. Be careful to hit only the pit with the knife blade. Twist blade slightly to remove pit. Scoop out meat with spoon.

Avocados need to be dipped in lemon juice to retain fresh appearance if they're used on top of dishes. Mayonnaise, butter or margarine may be used to coat exposed surfaces if avocado is not to be used soon.

BLACK- EYED PEA DIP

1/2 bell pepper, finely chopped
2 stalks celery, finely chopped
1 large onion, finely chopped
1 teaspoon black pepper
1-1/2 teaspoons hot pepper sauce, to taste
1/2 cup ketchup
1 teaspoon salt
1/8 teaspoon nutmeg
1/4 teaspoon cinnamon
1 teaspoon chicken bouillon powder
2 (15-ounce) cans black-eyed peas, drained
1 (15-ounce) can tomatoes
1 clove garlic, crushed
1 teaspoon sugar
1/2 cup bacon drippings
3 tablespoons cornstarch

PRE-GAME:
Combine first 9 ingredients. Heat in saucepan over low heat. Add bouillon, peas, tomatoes, garlic and sugar. Simmer 30 minutes. Combine bacon drippings with cornstarch and stir into pea mixture. Cook 10 minutes. Adjust seasonings. Stir.

FIRST QUARTER:
Serve hot with large corn chips or hunks of French bread.

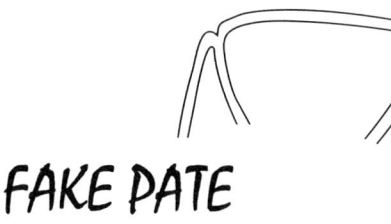

FAKE PATE

1 pound liverwurst (or braunschweiger)
2 packages Green Onion Dip Mix
1 teaspoon sugar
2 teaspoons water
1 tablespoon garlic spread
2 (3-ounce) packages cream cheese
1 tablespoon milk
1/8 teaspoon hot pepper sauce
Parsley, minced

PRE-GAME:

Mash liverwurst or braunschweiger (which is smoked liverwurst).
Combine dip mix, sugar and water. Add liverwurst; blend thoroughly.
Shape into a mound.
Cream garlic spread with cream cheese. Add milk and hot pepper sauce.
Spread cream mixture over liverwurst. Chill.
Garnish with parsley.

FIRST QUARTER:

Serve with rye crackers or melba rounds.

NICKEL DEFENSE DIP

2 large tomatoes, peeled
2 large avocados
12 green onions, chopped
3 tablespoons wine vinegar
1 tablespoon salad oil

PRE-GAME:

Cut tomatoes and avocados in small cubes. Mix with remaining ingredients.
Toss gently until well mixed. Salt and pepper optional.

FIRST QUARTER:

Serve with tortilla chips.

Note: These 5 ingredients tossed together make a nice change from guacamole.

THE FAKE
When an offensive player simulates or "fakes" possession of the ball in order to trick the defense.

NICKEL DEFENSE
Look for a 5th defensive back, replacing a linebacker, on a potential passing down. It's preventative defense against the pass.

PEANUTTY DIP WITH FRUIT

1 cup peanut butter
1 pint sour cream
1 tablespoon horseradish
1 teaspoon hot prepared mustard

PRE-GAME:
DIP: Blend ingredients.
Choose fruits in season: apples, bananas, grapes, pears or strawberries are good with this dip.
Slice fruit. Dip in lemon juice as needed to prevent discoloration. Refrigerate.
Arrange fruit on platter and serve dip in attractive bowl.

BASIC T FORMATION
Offensive backfield formation in which the fullback lines up 3-4 yards behind the quarterback. Two half backs line up on either side of the fullback.

BASIC DILL DIP

1 cup sour cream
1 cup mayonnaise
3 tablespoons fresh dill
1 tablespoon beau monde
1 tablespoon fresh parsley, minced
1 tablespoon green onions

PRE-GAME:
Mix ingredients thoroughly. Chill.
Prepare fresh vegetables: (Select some of the following.)

Bell Peppers - green, red, orange	Zucchini	Asparagus Spears
Cherry Tomatoes	Jicama	Green Beans
Celery	Turnips	Snow Peas
Cauliflower	Carrots	Button Mushrooms
Broccoli	Cucumbers	Radishes

FIRST QUARTER:
Serve dip surrounded by vegetables.

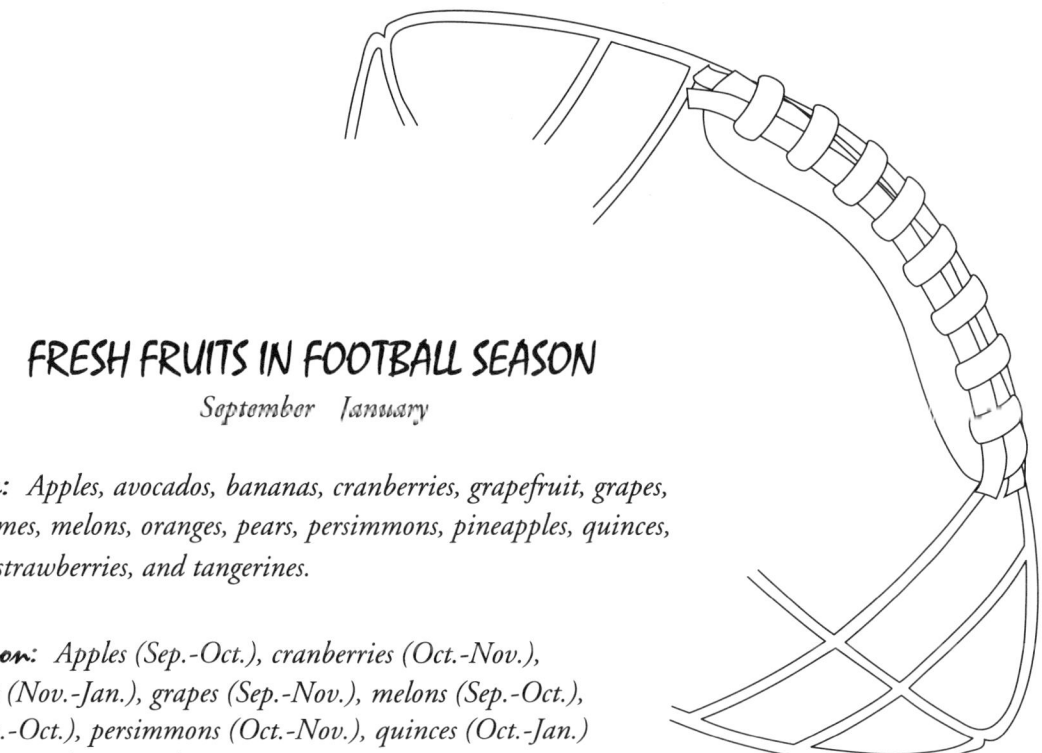

FRESH FRUITS IN FOOTBALL SEASON
September–January

Available: Apples, avocados, bananas, cranberries, grapefruit, grapes, lemons, limes, melons, oranges, pears, persimmons, pineapples, quinces, rhubarb, strawberries, and tangerines.

Peak Season: Apples (Sep.-Oct.), cranberries (Oct.-Nov.), grapefruit (Nov.-Jan.), grapes (Sep.-Nov.), melons (Sep.-Oct.), pears (Sep.-Oct.), persimmons (Oct.-Nov.), quinces (Oct.-Jan.) and tangerines (Dec.-Jan.).

FRESH VEGETABLES IN FOOTBALL SEASON
September-January

Available: Green beans, broccoli, cabbage, carrots, celery, eggplant, jicama, leeks, mushrooms, onions, peppers, potatoes, pumpkins (Sep.-Nov.), radishes, spinach, summer squash, tomatoes, watercress, waxed beans and winter squash (Sep.-Nov.).

Peak season: Broccoli, brussels sprouts (Oct.-Dec.), cauliflower (Oct.-Nov.), celery, endive (Nov.-Jan.), escarole (Oct.), green peppers (Sep.-Oct.), mushrooms (Nov.-Dec.), parsnips, potatoes, tomatoes (Sep.-Oct.) and winter squash (Oct.).

🏈 THE SCORE 🏈

There are four possible scores—6, 1, 3, or 2.

    6 points - Touchdown
    1 point   - Point after touchdown
    3 points - Field goal
    2 points - Safety

A *touchdown* is scored when a player carries the ball into the end zone by running with the ball or by catching a pass in the end zone.

The *point-after* can occur as a run, a pass or a place kick.

A *field goal* is scored when a player kicks the ball through the uprights of the opponent's goal. This may be done by a place kick or drop kick.

The most infrequent score is a *safety*. This score results when an offensive player is tackled or ruled down in his own end zone.

OYSTER FRITTERS

1 large jar oysters, drained
3-1/2 cups flour
2 teaspoons seafood seasoning
1 teaspoon black pepper
1 teaspoon salt
3 green onions, chopped

1/2 teaspoon baking powder
2 cloves garlic, chopped
2 teaspoons garlic powder
2 tablespoons chopped parsley
1 teaspoon coarse black pepper
2 cups or more beer

PRE-GAME:
Drain oysters well. Mix 1 cup flour with seafood seasoning, pepper and salt. Roll oysters in seasoned flour mixture. Set aside.
Blend remaining ingredients into a batter. Dip oysters in batter mix.
Deep-fry at 380 degrees for 2 minutes or until browned and crispy.
Drain on paper towels.

FIRST QUARTER:
May need to be reheated before serving.

CRAB-STUFFED CHEESE PUFFS

1 cup water
1/2 cup margarine
1/4 teaspoon salt
1 cup flour
4 eggs
3/4 cup cheese (Jarlsberg, cheddar, Muenster), shredded

Seafood

CRAB FILLING

1 (6-ounce) package frozen crab, thawed and flaked (or imitation crab)
1 cup cheese (Jarlsberg, cheddar, Muenster), shredded
1/2 cup sour cream
1/4 cup chutney, minced
1/4 cup green pepper, minced
1/4 teaspoon curry powder

PRE-GAME:
Combine water, margarine and salt in saucepan.
Bring to a full boil.
Add flour all at once and cook, stirring until
mixture forms a ball.
Reduce heat if necessary. Remove from heat; add beaten
eggs one at a time. Beat mixture well after each addition.
Mix in cheese.
Drop by tablespoons onto ungreased cookie sheet.
Bake at 400 degrees for 35 minutes or until golden.
Remove from oven. Turn off oven. Make a small slit in each puff.
Return puffs to oven for 10 minutes.
Remove to wire rack to cool.
Stuff with crab filling.

FILLING:
Blend all ingredients together.

Yield: 24 large puffs or 36 medium puffs

Surimi is the name sometimes given to imitation seafood. Actually, surimi is a colorless, odorless paste made from white fish protein. It is a stabilizer in many foods—e.g. bologna. When you see a product labeled "Imitation King Crab (Krab)" it may be pollock or other white fish enhanced with crab juice. Imitation shrimp actually has shrimp in combination with other white fish.

PICKLED SALMON

1 earthenware crock
1 canning jar
Salmon fillets, cut into 2" strips
Kosher salt

Brown sugar
For each canning jar: 1 sliced onion
olive oil
vinegar

PICKLING JUICE

1 quart vinegar
1 quart water
2 tablespoons salt

1 tablespoon brown sugar
1 bottle pickling spices
(wrapped in cheesecloth)

PRE-GAME:
Roll salmon fillets first in kosher salt and then brown sugar.
In an earthenware crock, layer salmon in a criss-cross pattern.
Cover with a plate and weight down to make a tight seal.
Set aside 30-40 hours.
Remove fish from crock, pour out brine; wash crock.
Return fish to crock. Pour in pickling spice mixture to cover.
Set aside 7-8 days.
Remove fish from crock; cut off skin and slice salmon into bite-size pieces.
Layer fish and onion slices in sterilized canning jar(s). Repeat.
Cover with mixture of half olive oil and half vinegar.
Refrigerate.

PICKLING JUICE: Mix ingredients together. (Do not use a metal pot.)

FIRST QUARTER:
Serve pickled salmon with a variety of crackers or spear with toothpicks and arrange atop greens.

SPEARING
A player may not dive head-first into a downed or tackled player. The penalty is 15 yards and automatic first down.

CRAB DIP IN SHEEPHERDER BREAD

- 1 loaf unsliced Sheepherder bread
- 1 can white crab meat with juice or 1 (8-ounce) package imitation crab
- 1 (8-ounce) package cream cheese
- 7 green onions, chopped fine
- 2 cups extra sharp cheddar cheese (3/4 pound)
- 5 tablespoons Worcestershire sauce
- 1 cup sour cream
- 1/2 teaspoon Tabasco sauce

PRE-GAME:
Cut top from Sheepherder bread and scoop out inside—saving bread.
Cube into small pieces and toast later.
Mix remaining ingredients. Place in bread shells. Top with bread lid.
Wrap in heavy-duty foil.
Bake at 350 degrees for 1-1/2 hours.
If it is not to be served in a few hours, refrigerate.

FIRST QUARTER:
You may wish to reheat in oven if bread has been refrigerated earlier.

CRAB MOLD

- 1 package unflavored gelatin
- 1 tablespoon water
- 1 can cream of mushroom soup
- 1 (8-ounce) package cream cheese, softened
- 6-12 ounces crab meat or imitation crab
- 1 cup mayonnaise
- 1 cup celery, chopped
- 1 cup green onions, chopped
- Juice of 1/2 lemon
- 2 teaspoons fresh chives
- 1 teaspoon dill
- 2 teaspoons parsley

PRE-GAME:
Dissolve gelatin in water and combine with soup and cheese.
Beat mixture until well blended; cool.
In separate bowl mix remaining ingredients. Add to cooled mixture.
Spray mold. Place mixture in mold; refrigerate 12 hours or more.

FIRST QUARTER:
Serve with crackers or crudites.

DRESSED SHRIMP

2 tablespoons olive oil
1 tablespoon lemon juice
2 tablespoons water
1/2 cup Italian seasoned
   bread crumbs
2 teaspoons garlic salt

Dash pepper
2 teaspoons parsley
1 pound medium or
   large fresh shrimp
   (shelled and deveined)

PRE-GAME:
In small bowl combine oil, lemon juice and water.
In another bowl mix bread crumbs, garlic salt, pepper and parsley.
Towel-dry shrimp. Dip each shrimp in oil mixture,
then roll in bread crumb mixture to coat.
Arrange breaded shrimp in a single layer on a foil-lined
cookie sheet. Cover and refrigerate.

FIRST QUARTER:
Preheat broiler and place pan about 4 inches from heat. Broil 3 minutes.
Turn and broil 3 minutes on other side until browned.

UNDRESSED SHRIMP

1-1/2 pounds medium shrimp,
   cooked, peeled and deveined
1/2 cup safflower oil
1/2 cup olive oil
1/2 cup wine vinegar
1 egg, beaten

2 tablespoons prepared mustard
2 tablespoons chives, minced
2 tablespoons green onions,
   thinly sliced
1/2 teaspoon salt
1/2 teaspoon sugar
1/4 teaspoon freshly ground pepper

PRE-GAME:
Whisk oils with vinegar. Add remaining ingredients and whisk.
Place shrimp in rectangular glass dish. Pour ingredients over shrimp.
Refrigerate 8 hours or more (up to 2 days). Drain before serving.

FIRST QUARTER:
Serve shrimp on a bed of lettuce.

FIRST AND TEN MUSSELS

24 mussels

MARINADE

3 tablespoons sesame oil
3 tablespoons rice vinegar
1 clove garlic, minced
1/4 cup green pepper, thinly sliced
1/4 cup sweet red pepper, thinly sliced
3 tablespoons parsley

3 tablespoons green onions, sliced, plus 2" of the green tops
1/4 teaspoon ginger
3/4 teaspoon Chinese chili sauce
1 teaspoon soy sauce

PRE-GAME:
Clean mussels with a knife and scouring pad to scrape off all crusty matter sticking to the shells. Wash well with stiff brush. Pull or cut off the beards (a stringy black thread along the shell).

Fill a large pot with water and add 1 teaspoon salt. Bring to a rolling boil; add mussels and cover. When mussels open (in approximately 5 minutes) transfer to a colander to cool; refrigerate.

Cook the unopened mussels a while longer. If they do not open after 8-10 minutes, they are dead and should be discarded.

MARINADE: Whisk oils and vinegar. Add garlic, peppers, parsley, green onions, ginger, chili sauce and soy sauce; mix well.

Remove mussels from their shells; marinate 2 hours. Refrigerate.

Mix mussel shells with 3 tablespoons olive oil and toss carefully so as to not detach the shell halves.

Arrange shells on a platter. Insert mussel meat. Cover with plastic wrap; refrigerate up to 6 hours before serving.

FIRST QUARTER:
Serve chilled.

FIRST AND TEN
A team has four downs total to gain 10 yards. They retain possession until they score, have a turnover or interception or fail to make 10 yards and a new first down.

GRAVLAX

7-8 pounds salmon, center-cut, one piece
2/3 cup salt
3/4 cup sugar
2 tablespoons freshly ground white pepper
3 teaspoons allspice, coarsely ground
2 cups fresh dill
1-1/2 cups Cognac

PRE-GAME:
Salmon should be boned and filleted. Skin optional.
Preferably it should be a salt-water, red (sockeye)
or silver salmon.
Place salmon in flat glass dish.
Mix ingredients and pour over salmon.
Press spices into salmon.
Cover with plastic wrap and weight down with heavy object.
Refrigerate 36-48 hours or longer. Turn three times a day.
Scrape off spices and wipe dry. Chill.

FIRST QUARTER:
Slice salmon on bias. Serve with cream cheese, toasted bagels, capers or rye rounds.

CLAM SPREAD

1 can minced clams, drained
1/2 pound fresh mushrooms
2 tablespoons margarine
1 (8-ounce) package cream cheese
1 teaspoon soy sauce
1 teaspoon Worcestershire sauce
1 teaspoon lemon juice
1 teaspoon savory
1 small onion, chopped

PRE-GAME:
Saute mushrooms and margarine.
Mix all ingredients and heat in a double boiler until mixture is easy to stir.

FIRST QUARTER:
Serve warm with garlic rounds or melba toast.

SMOKED SALMON

1 salmon fillet, rib bones removed
1/2 cup kosher salt
  or other iodine-free salt
1 gallon water
1 cup brown sugar
1/4 cup molasses
cottonwood or birch chips

PRE-GAME:
Cut salmon fillets lengthwise.
Each strip should be about 1-1/4" thick on the side.

BRINE: Add kosher salt, brown sugar and molasses to each gallon of water. Stir brine for 10 minutes or more making sure salt and sugar are dissolved. Place salmon in brine; soak 5 to 6 hours.
To smoke: remove salmon from brine; hang to dry for 12 to 15 hours in 74-76 degree temperature; use fan or other device to circulate air. Cold-smoke for 1 to 2 hours, using dry cottonwood or birch chips.

CANNED SALMON:
Pressure-cook at 10 PSI for 90 minutes after cutting and packing strips in sterilized wide-mouth canning jars.
Add to each jar before sealing:
   1/4 teaspoon white pepper or jalapeño pepper
   pinch dill weed
   3 tablespoons tomato juice

FIRST QUARTER:
Smoked salmon is so good it can stand alone as an appetizer, but you may also serve it with crackers, garlic toast rounds or bagels and cream cheese.

THE CONVERSION

The conversion is another name for the 1-point scoring attempt made after a touchdown. It may also be called the "try-for-point" score. The defensive team can never score on the conversion. The ball is ruled dead as soon as the defense gets possession or the kick is blocked.

SESAME CHICKEN HONEY DIP

1/2 cup mayonnaise
1 teaspoon dry mustard
1 teaspoon instant minced onion
1/2 cup dry bread crumbs
1/4 cup sesame seeds
2 cups cubed cooked chicken or turkey

HONEY DIP

1/2 cup mayonnaise
1 tablespoon honey

PRE-GAME:
Mix first three ingredients; set aside.
Mix crumbs and sesame seeds.
Coat chicken with mayonnaise mixture, then crumb mixture.
Place chicken on baking sheet. Bake at 425 degrees for 12-15 minutes or until lightly browned.

HONEY DIP: Mix mayonnaise and honey.

FIRST QUARTER:
Heat honey dip and serve warm. Chicken pieces may be dipped in the honey or it may be drizzled over the chicken and served with crackers.

Note: Sesame Chicken can convert to luncheon or dinner entree.

PARTY BLITZ MEATBALLS

1 pound ground beef
3/4 teaspoon salt
1/2 teaspoon seasoned pepper
1 tablespoon onions, chopped
1/2 cup bread crumbs
1/4 cup milk
Flour
Olive oil

SAUCE

6 tablespoons unsulphured molasses
6 tablespoons prepared mustard
6 tablespoons white vinegar
1/2 cup ketchup
1/2 teaspoon thyme

PRE-GAME:
Mix beef with salt, pepper, onions, bread crumbs and milk. Form into 3/4" balls. Roll in flour and brown in oil.

SAUCE: Combine all ingredients for sauce and blend until smooth. Pour sauce over meatballs. Simmer; stir occasionally until sauce thickens and balls are glazed.

FIRST QUARTER:
Heat and serve.

Note: If frozen, reheat in 300-degree oven for 1 hour. Convert this to an entree by forming larger meatballs. Serve atop noodles.

The purpose of the blitz is to sack the quarterback. This is a surprise defensive maneuver in which one or more linebackers and/or safeties charges across the line of scrimmage.

TWENTY-YARD LINE TERIYAKI CHICKEN WINGS

3-1/2 - 4 pounds drummettes or chicken wings

MARINADE

1-1/2 cups soy sauce
1/3-3/4 cup brown sugar
1/3-1/2 cup ketchup
1 large onion, sliced

2-3 garlic cloves, crushed
1-1/2" ginger root, minced
2 tablespoons sesame seeds

PRE-GAME:

Prepare marinade. Marinate chicken several hours. Refrigerate. Place foil in broiler pan. Cook chicken at 350 degrees until done, approximately 40 minutes.
Baste after 20 minutes with additional marinade.

Note: Convert this to an entree by marinating larger chicken pieces.

TOUCHBACK
Play in which the ball is dead in the end zone. The impetus must derive from the opponent. The ball is brought out to the 20-yard line.

STEAK TARTARE

2 pounds extra lean ground sirloin steak
1/2 onion, finely chopped
1/2 cup capers, drained
8 anchovy fillets, finely chopped

4 egg yolks
1 teaspoon salt
1/8 teaspoon freshly ground pepper
1/4 cup finely chopped watercress
   (if unavailable, use butter lettuce)

PRE-GAME:
Have your butcher intentionally grind sirloin steak twice.
Mix all ingredients very thoroughly. (Use plastic gloves to mix the ingredients or a plastic bag on each hand.)
Spray a jelly mold or bowl with non-stick spray.
Press meat mixture into bowl.
Chill 2-3 hours and unmold.

FIRST QUARTER:
Serve with pumpernickel, party rye or melba rounds.

Note: Serve atop lettuce and this tartare converts to a luncheon dish.

INTENTIONAL GROUNDING

An infraction in which the passer avoids being tackled behind the line of scrimmage so he throws an incomplete pass. It may be thrown into the ground, out of bounds or beyond a receiver.

SALADS - BOWLS STADIUMS

In 1922 the American Professional Football Association changed its name to the National Football League. Over the next twenty years the NFL faced a few challenges from others trying to form a league. The most successful of the early attempts was the All-American Football Conference. This league produced the Cleveland Browns, the San Francisco 49ers and the Baltimore Colts. After four years, the AAFC and the NFL waged a costly war. Finally, after the 1949 season, the AAFC agreed to the NFL's terms for a merger.

In 1960, the fourth American Football League was born. It presented the most serious challenger to the NFL. Finally, in 1966, a merger between the AFL and the NFL was agreed upon. Beginning in 1970, the AFL would be known as the American Football Conference and the NFL would become the National Football Conference. Together the two conferences would make up the National Football League.

Also, as part of the merger agreement, beginning with the 1966 season, an annual Championship Game between the AFC and the NFL would be played. This annual Championship Game is now known as the Super Bowl.

Let's take a look at some teams in the NFL and the bowls or stadiums, where they play.

SALADS

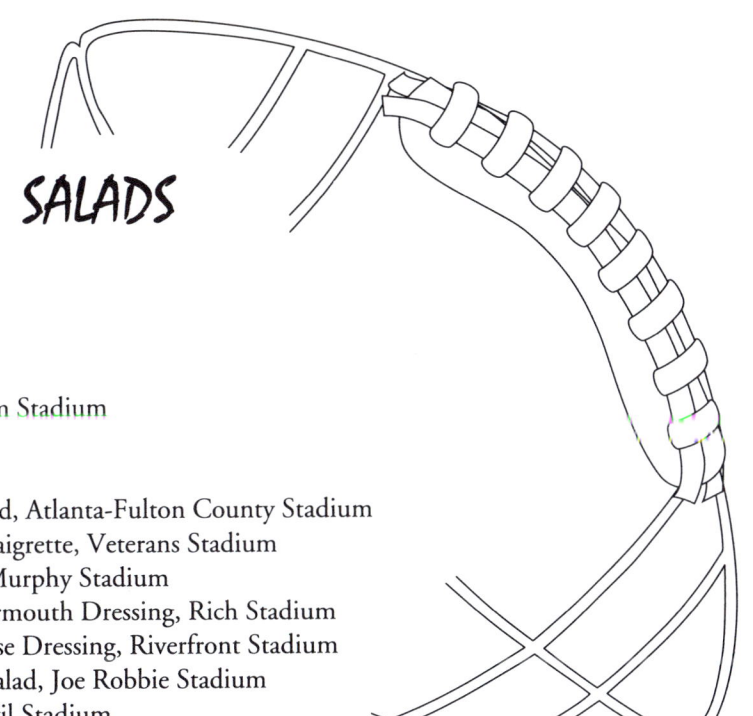

GREEN SALADS

Avocado-Citrus Salad, Anaheim Stadium
Caesar Salad, Superdome
Cobb Salad, RFK Stadium
Feta, Olives with Pine Nut Salad, Atlanta-Fulton County Stadium
Gruyere and Walnut Salad Vinaigrette, Veterans Stadium
Monterey Jack Melange, Jack Murphy Stadium
Red Tip Lettuce Salad with Vermouth Dressing, Rich Stadium
Romaine Salad with Blue Cheese Dressing, Riverfront Stadium
Romano, Romaine, Red Leaf Salad, Joe Robbie Stadium
Special Spinach Salad, Sun Devil Stadium
Tex Mex Caesar Salad, Texas Stadium
"Three R"— Romaine, Raisin and Red Dressing, Three Rivers Stadium
Two-Team Meadowlands Garden State Salad, Giants Stadium,

PASTA SALADS

Antipasta Salad, Astrodome
Pasta/Sausage Salad, Pontiac Silverdome
Peppers and Pickle Pasta Salad, Candlestick Park

GELATIN SALAD

Aspic Salad, Arrowhead Stadium

VEGETABLE SALADS

Cabbage Crunch Salad, Cleveland Stadium
Cauliflower/Broccoli Salad, Foxboro Stadium
Coliseum Coleslaw, Memorial Coliseum
Peas and Cashews Crunch Salad, Kingdome

SPECIALTY SALADS

LAYERED SALAD
Vegetable Layered Salad, Lambeau Field
ORIENTAL
Chinese Chicken and Cilantro Salad, H. H. H. Metrodome
FRUIT
24-Hour Cherry Salad, Hoosier Dome
SEAFOOD
Tomato, Shrimp and Avocado Salad, Tampa Stadium

STADIUM GREENS

Grass: AFC: *Cleveland Stadium, Mile-High Stadium, Los Angeles Memorial Coliseum , *Joe Robbie Stadium, Foxboro Stadium and Jack Murphy Stadium.

NFC: *Atlanta-Fulton County Stadium, Soldier Field, Lambeau Field and Milwaukee County Stadium, Anaheim Stadium, Sun Devil Stadium, Candlestick Park and Tampa Stadium.

Astroturf: AFC: Rich Stadium, Riverfront Stadium, Astrodome, Hoosier Dome, Arrowhead Stadium, Giants Stadium, Three Rivers Stadium and Kingdome

NFC: Texas Stadium, Pontiac Silverdome, H.H.H. Metrodome, Louisiana Superdome, Giants Stadium and Veterans Stadium.

AstroTurf

In 1966, baseball players in the Houston Astrodome first recognized a problem. They were unable to see high fly balls against the glass dome. The dome was darkened, enabling players to see the ball, but then the grass died.

In response to the problem, Monsanto Corporation developed a new surface for the Astrodome. The parent company claims that AstroTurf, the brand name, is not a synthetic turf. It's a knitted nylon fabric—textured with no directionality.

Astroturf is a layer of carpet on top of several thicknesses of padding and six feet of asphalt. Some stadiums have AstroTurf equipped with zippers in order to add or subtract pieces of turf. (Baseball needs a larger field than football). Others may have pieces attached with a velcro-like fabric. A few stadiums have AstroTurf, Magic Carpet. Through a system of air vents the new surface can be lifted and stored in just a few hours, revealing another surface beneath.

*These stadiums have grass (PAT)—grass with a mixture of sand. It's helpful for drainage.

SALAD GREENS

Butterhead lettuce (Bibb, Boston and limestone). These are delicate, almost buttery-flavor lettuces.

Chicory. This curly salad green should be mixed with other greens. It imparts a slightly bitter taste.

Endive. Probably the most expensive salad green. It has a delicate, but distinct flavor.

Iceberg or head lettuce. Choose ones that are green, not light, in color. The heads should be compact. This lettuce is composed mostly of water and does not contain the vitamins and minerals of the darker green lettuce-family members. It stays crisper longer than some other types of lettuce.

Red leaf lettuce. A mild-flavored lettuce distinguished by its ruffled leaves.

Romaine. Usually dark to medium green in color, romaine's crisp leaves stand up well to heavy dressings.

Watercress. These small green leaves should be paired with other salad greens prior to serving because watercress wilts easily with the addition of dressing.

To clean several heads of lettuce: Cut core or stem out of the head and separate leaves. Fill sink with cold water and place leaves of one head of lettuce in sink. Gently swish leaves in the water. Allow to rest a few minutes to enable gritty matter to sink down. Lift out and run cold water and on each leaf. Gather head together and shake out excess water. Dry lettuce.

To dry: Use a salad spinner to remove excess water. Wrap in a clean towel and store in plastic bag in refrigerator. For longer storage, up to 2 days, wrap a single layer of leaves between paper towels and place on tray. Cover with plastic wrap.

AVOCADO CITRUS SALAD

2 heads red leaf lettuce
1 grapefruit, peeled and sliced
2 oranges, peeled and sliced

2 avocados, peeled and sliced length-wise
Lemon juice
Dash salt

HONEY-SEED DRESSING

1/3 to 1/2 cup toasted sesame seeds
1/2 cup oil
1/2 cup honey
2 tablespoons vinegar

1/2 teaspoon dry mustard
1/2 teaspoon paprika
1/8 teaspoon salt
1/2 teaspoon celery seed

PRE-GAME:
Tear leaf lettuce into bite-size pieces.
Peel and remove membrane from grapefruit and oranges.
Section fruit. Slice sections in thirds or halves.
Refrigerate.

DRESSING:
Toast sesame seeds in 200-degree oven, stirring frequently.
Whisk oil and honey together. Add vinegar and whisk again.
Add remaining ingredients including the cooled sesame seeds. Place in quart jar and refrigerate.

HALF-TIME:
Sprinkle avocado slices with lemon juice and salt.
Mix greens and dressing. Add fruit and toss again with chopped avocados (or use sliced avocados as garnish atop salad.)

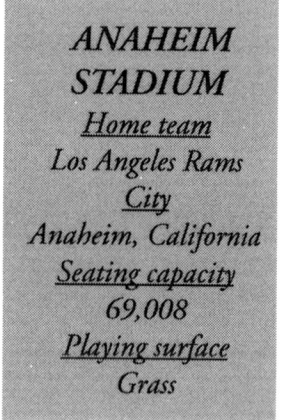

ANAHEIM STADIUM
Home team
Los Angeles Rams
City
Anaheim, California
Seating capacity
69,008
Playing surface
Grass

FETA, OLIVES & PINE NUT SALAD

1-1/2 heads, lettuce
1 pound Feta cheese
1 cucumber, peeled, sliced
2 cups cherry tomatoes, sliced
3 ounces small Calamata (Greek) black olives, pitted, sliced
5 ounces Naphlion (Greek) green olives, pitted, sliced
1/2 bell pepper, diced
4 green onions, finely chopped
1/2 cup pine nuts
1 avocado, pitted, peeled, sliced

DRESSING

7 tablespoons olive oil
3 tablespoons lemon juice
1/8 teaspoon oregano
Salt and pepper

PRE-GAME:
Wash lettuce and pat dry.
Mix next 7 ingredients and half the pine nuts with half the dressing. Refrigerate.

DRESSING: Whisk oil and vinegar. Add spices.

HALF-TIME:
Toss greens with dressing.
Layer greens on oblong platter.
Arrange ingredients atop greens. Sprinkle additional dressing over salad. Top with avocado slices. Sprinkle remaining pine nuts.

ATLANTA FULTON COUNTY STADIUM
Home team
Atlanta Falcons
City
Atlanta, Georgia
Seating capacity
59,643
Playing surface
Grass (PAT)

ANTIPASTA SALAD

3/4 cup red bell peppers, diced
1 (20-ounce) can red kidney beans, drained
1 (20-ounce) can chick peas (garbanzo beans), drained
2 ounces salami, sliced in 1/4" pieces
2 ounces ham, sliced in 1/4" strips
2 jars marinated artichokes
2 jars marinated mushrooms

MARINADE

1/3 cup olive oil
2 tablespoons red wine vinegar
1/2 teaspoon salt
1/2 teaspoon onion powder
1/4 teaspoon garlic powder
1/8 teaspoon black pepper
1/2 teaspoon tarragon leaves (optional)

PRE-GAME:

Saute red pepper in 1 teaspoon olive oil until soft. Drain on paper towels. Mix red pepper with remaining ingredients.
MARINADE: Whisk oil and vinegar. Add remaining spices and whisk again. Pour marinade over all ingredients and mix well. Cover bowl; refrigerate at least two hours. (Overnight is even better.)

HALF-TIME:

Serve on top of lettuce leaves.

ASTRODOME
Home team
Houston Oilers
City
Houston, Texas
Seating capacity
60,502
Playing surface
AstroTurf-8

CAULIFLOWER/BROCCOLI SALAD

- 1 bunch broccoli
- 1 bunch cauliflower
- 15 strips bacon, cooked and crumbled
- 2 cups purple onion, finely chopped
- 2 cups raisins

DRESSING

- 2 cups mayonnaise
- 4 tablespoons sugar
- 4 tablespoons vinegar

PRE-GAME:
Break broccoli and cauliflower into very small flowerets.
Mix broccoli, cauliflower, bacon, onion and raisins.
DRESSING: Mix ingredients. Pour dressing over salad ingredients and toss lightly. Refrigerate at least one hour.

ASPIC SALAD

- 1 (3-ounce) package lemon-flavored gelatin
- 1-1/4 cups hot water
- 1 (8-ounce) can tomato sauce
- 1-1/2 tablespoons white vinegar
- 1/2 teaspoon salt
- 1/4 cup celery, minced
- 1/4 cup stuffed green olives, sliced
- 2 tablespoons grated onion
- 1 can small shrimp, drained
- dash—Tabasco sauce, pepper, ground cloves, celery seasoning and cayenne pepper

PRE-GAME:
Dissolve gelatin in hot water.
Blend in remaining ingredients.
Spray a gelatin mold with non-stick spray; wipe off excess.
Pour ingredients into mold.
Chill until firm.

HALF-TIME:
Unmold onto a bed of lettuce. Garnish with mayonnaise (optional).

FOXBORO STADIUM
Home team
New England Patriots
City
Foxboro, Massachusetts
Seating capacity
60,794
Playing surface
Grass

ARROW HEAD STADIUM
Home team
Kansas City Chiefs
City
Kansas City, Missouri
Seating capacity
80,098
Playing surface
AstroTurf-8

CAESAR SALAD

2 large heads romaine lettuce, torn and chilled
1-2 coddled eggs
1/2 cup Parmesan cheese, freshly grated
2 cups croutons
Anchovies or anchovy paste

DRESSING

3/4 cup olive oil
1/2 teaspoon kosher salt
2 cloves garlic, crushed
1/4 teaspoon freshly ground black pepper
Juice of 1 lemon

PRE-GAME:
Rinse and pat lettuce dry. Discard large center rib and tear into bite-size pieces; cover and chill. Pre-season salad bowl.
DRESSING: In a separate bowl whisk remaining oil with salt, garlic, pepper and lemon.

HALF-TIME:
Place greens in seasoned bowl. Toss dressing and romaine lettuce together; coat greens thoroughly. Add coddled egg. (Pierce the large end of an egg with a push pin and carefully place egg in a pot of boiling water for 1 minute. Remove.) Toss greens. Add anchovies or anchovy paste (mashed with a small amount of olive oil or dressing). Add cheese and croutons tossing after each addition.

Pre-Season Salad Bowls:
Rub wooden bowl with kosher salt and a garlic half. This will perfume the lettuce leaves for added piquancy.

PRE-SEASON
Players attend their respective training camps starting in July. Returning veterans and rookies vie for starting positions or just making the team. The pre-season kicks off in August. Mandatory roster reductions occur prior to the season opener in September.

Teams may not exceed a 45-player limit. In the 1991 season a 46th player or third quarterback was allowed.

SUPERDOME
Home team
New Orleans Saints
City
New Orleans, Louisiana
Seating capacity
69,065
Playing surface
AstroTurf

ROMANO, ROMAINE, RED LEAF SALAD

2 heads romaine lettuce
1 head red leaf lettuce
1 tablespoon olive oil
2 cloves garlic, split
1/4 teaspoon salt
1 pound bacon, cooked, crumbled

2 tomatoes, cut-up
1/4 cup green onions, chopped
1 cup bean sprouts
1/2 cup fresh Romano cheese, grated
Homemade croutons

DRESSING

1 cup olive oil
1/4 cup lemon juice
1/2 teaspoon freshly ground pepper
1/4 teaspoon oregano
1 coddled egg (optional)

PRE-GAME:
Pre-season salad bowl. (see p. 56)
Place tomatoes, green onions and bean sprouts in bowl.
Add lettuce and toss with bacon.

DRESSING: In a separate bowl whisk coddled egg (see p. 56) vigorously. Add olive oil and lemon juice, whisk again. Add pepper and oregano. Store in a jar. Refrigerate.

SECOND QUARTER:
Toss greens with dressing. Add cheese and croutons.
Toss after each addition

Yield: 8-10 servings

JOE ROBBIE STADIUM
<u>Home team</u>
Miami Dolphins
<u>City</u>
Miami, Florida
<u>Seating capacity</u>
73,000
<u>Playing surface</u>
Grass

COLISEUM COLESLAW

1 head cabbage
1 medium onion, finely chopped
1 green pepper, seeded and finely chopped
1 tablespoon salt

1 cup cider vinegar
1 teaspoon celery seed
1 teaspoon mustard seed
3/4 cup sugar

PRE-GAME:

Quarter cabbage and remove core. Shred cabbage and cover 1 hour with cold water; drain. Combine cabbage, onion, green pepper and salt in large pot. Cover with boiling water and put on lid.
Allow to stand 1 hour. Drain in colander.
Return cabbage mixture to pot.
In separate bowl mix vinegar, celery seed, mustard seed and sugar (start with 1/2 cup and gradually add up to 3/4 cup.
Taste to make sure it doesn't become too sweet--for some, 3/4 cup sugar may be too much).
Pour over cabbage; refrigerate one day.

HALF-TIME:

Line salad bowl with lettuce and mound coleslaw in center.

Note: This makes a large quantity of coleslaw. Place whatever coleslaw you do not bring for football in wide mouth pickle or canning jars and refrigerate. Lasts 3-4 weeks.

MEMORIAL COLISEUM
Home team
Los Angeles Raiders
City
Los Angeles, California
Seating capacity
92,488 (largest in NFL)
Playing surface
Grass

GRUYERE, WALNUT SALAD AND VINAIGRETTE

2 cups lettuce—Bibb, butter, iceberg or leaf
1/2 cup walnuts, coarsely chopped
1/2 pound bacon, cooked and crumbled
1/2 cup Gruyere cheese, grated
1-1/2 cups croutons

VINAIGRETTE

1 cup olive oil
1/3 cup red wine vinegar
1 teaspoon seasoned salt or kosher salt
1/2 teaspoon seasoned pepper
1/2 teaspoon freshly ground black pepper
1/4 teaspoon garlic powder
1 tablespoon fresh parsley, chopped

PRE-GAME:
Rinse and pat lettuce dry. Tear into bite-size pieces; cover and chill.

DRESSING: Place olive oil and vinegar in a bowl and whisk together. Add salt, pepper, garlic powder and parsley to the olive oil and whisk again. Refrigerate.

HALF-TIME:
Whisk dressing and sprinkle over salad greens. Toss salad.
Add walnuts and bacon; toss well.
Add cheese and croutons; toss again.

VETERANS STADIUM
Home team
Philadelphia Eagles
City
Philadelphia, Pennsylvania
Seating capacity
65,356
Playing surface
AstroTurf-8

TWO-TEAM MEADOWLANDS GARDEN STATE SALAD

1 head Bibb lettuce
1 head endive
1 bunch watercress
8-10 button mushrooms, sliced

1 cucumber, peeled
10 cherry tomatoes, sliced
1 red bell pepper, thinly sliced
1 tablespoon sesame seeds

DRESSING

1 cup olive oil
1 tablespoon red wine vinegar
Juice of 1 lemon.
1 egg, coddled
1 clove garlic, minced

1/2 teaspoon salt
1 teaspoon Dijon mustard
1 tablespoon hot pepper sauce
3 tablespoons sour cream
2 teaspoons tomato sauce

GIANTS' STADIUM
Home Team
New York Giants
New York Jets
City
East Rutherford, New Jersey
Seating capacity
77,152
Playing surface
AstroTurf

PRE-GAME:
Wash greens and pat dry. Tear Bibb lettuce into bite-size pieces. Prepare mushrooms, cucumber, tomatoes and red pepper.

DRESSING: Whisk oil with vinegar. In a separate dish, blend lemon juice and egg yolk. Combine all dressing ingredients. Whisk again.

HALF-TIME:
Toss salad and vegetables with dressing.
Sprinkle with sesame seeds

CHINESE CHICKEN AND CILANTRO SALAD

4 chicken breasts
Garlic salt

MARINADE

1 cup sherry
1/2 teaspoon ginger
1/4 cup soy sauce
1/4 teaspoon garlic powder

SALAD

Flour
Won ton skins
2 green onions
2 teaspoons sesame seeds
1/2 cup cilantro or parsley
1 head lettuce, cleaned and torn into bite size pieces

DRESSING

1/4 cup oil
2 tablespoons rice vinegar
2 tablespoons sugar
1 teaspoon salt
1/4 teaspoon pepper
1 tablespoon sesame seeds

PRE-GAME:

MARINADE: Mix all ingredients.
Clean and pat dry chicken breasts. (Do not remove skin.)
Sprinkle with garlic salt. Cover with marinade and place in refrigerator overnight.
Coat chicken lightly with flour.
Fry chicken until done. Drain on paper towels.
Fry won ton skins until crisp, approximately 10 seconds.
Dry on paper towels. When dry, crush. Place in brown bag.
Shred chicken. Use skin (if desired).

DRESSING: Mix all ingredients; refrigerate.

HALF-TIME:

Toss chicken with onions, sesame seeds, cilantro or parsley and lettuce.
Add dressing and toss with won tons.

HUBERT H. HUMPHREY METRODOME
Home team
Minnesota Vikings
City
Minneapolis, Minnesota
Seating capacity
63,000
Playing surface
AstroTurf

PEPPERS AND PICKLE PASTA SALAD

1 (18-ounce) package tri-colored corkscrew macaroni or fusili
1 teaspoon salt
2 teaspoons olive oil

VEGETABLES

1 bell pepper, finely diced
1/2 red pepper, finely diced
1 cup sweet pickles, diced (approximately 6)
1 purple onion, finely chopped
1 large tomato, finely diced

DRESSING

1-1/2 cups mayonnaise
1/2 cup sour cream
1/4 cup milk
2 teaspoons beef bouillon powder
1 tablespoon pickle juice
2 teaspoons lemon juice
Dash of balsamic vinegar
1 teaspoon salt
1/8 teaspoon freshly ground pepper
2-1/2 teaspoons dill weed
3 hard-boiled eggs, chopped

PRE-GAME:
Bring water to rolling boil; add salt and small amount of olive oil. Add pasta maintaining the boil. Stir often. When tender, drain and rinse well with cold water. Place in large mixing bowl.
Prepare vegetables.

DRESSING: Mix mayonnaise, sour cream, milk, bouillon, pickle juice, lemon juice, vinegar, salt, pepper and dill.

Pour dressing over cooled pasta. Add diced vegetables and pickles. Reserve 2 tablespoons of onions and peppers for garnish (optional). Add more vinegar to taste. Garnish with eggs.
Refrigerate covered.

Yield: 12 servings

CANDLESTICK PARK
Home team
San Francisco 49ers
City
San Francisco, California
Seating capacity
65,729
Playing surface
Grass

24-HOUR CHERRY SALAD

2 cups whole sweet cherries
1 egg
2 tablespoons lemon juice
2 tablespoons sugar
Pinch salt

1/2 cup whipping cream
1 (16-ounce) can fruit cocktail, drained
3/4 cup mandarin or fresh orange sections
3/4 cup miniature marshmallows, halved
Mayonnaise (1 teaspoon per slice)

PRE-GAME:
Stem and pit cherries. Reserve 6 for garnish.
In double boiler, beat egg. Add lemon juice, sugar and salt.
Stir while cooking over hot water. When thick, remove. Cool.
Whip cream. Fold into cooled egg mixture.
Drain cherries, fruit cocktail and orange sections.
Combine with whipped cream mixture and marshmallows.
Refrigerate 24 hours or more.

HALF-TIME:
Slice and serve on lettuce greens. Garnish each serving with mayonnaise. Top with a cherry.

Yield: 6 servings

HOOSIER DOME
Home team
Indianapolis Colts
City
Indianapolis, Indiana
Seating capacity
60,127
Playing surface
AstroTurf

CABBAGE CRUNCH SALAD

1-1/2 heads of cabbage, medium size, shredded
2/3 cup fresh parsley, chopped
5-6 green onions, chopped
2 cups frozen peas, defrosted
1-1/2 cups Spanish peanuts
Mayonnaise

PRE-GAME:
Quarter cabbage, remove core and shred. Place in bowl.
Mix parsley, green onions, peas (defrost, but do not cook) and peanuts.
Mix in cabbage and add mayonnaise to combine. Chill.

Note: Baby shrimp, chicken, lamb, beef and pork can be added to this salad.

CLEVELAND STADIUM
Home team
Cleveland Browns
City
Cleveland, Ohio
Seating capacity
80,098
Playing surface
Grass

VEGETABLE LAYERED SALAD

1/2 head romaine lettuce
1 (16-ounce) can red kidney beans, drained
1 cup walnuts, chopped
12 fresh mushrooms, thinly sliced
1 red onion, thinly sliced in rings
1 (2.4-ounce) can pitted black olives, drained
1 large cucumber, thinly sliced
1 cup walnut halves, (optional)

DRESSING

1 (16-ounce) carton sour cream
4 tablespoons Parmesan cheese
1 tablespoon fresh dill, chopped (or 1-2 teaspoons dried dill)
1/3 cup fresh parsley, chopped
garlic salt and seasoning salt to taste

PRE-GAME:
Tear lettuce into bite-size pieces. Layer ingredients (preferably in a glass bowl) in the above order.

DRESSING: Mix all ingredients. Pour dressing over cucumber slices. Do not mix.

Yield: 6-8 servings

Note: Garnish top with 1 cup walnut halves.

LAMBEAU FIELD
Home team
Green Bay Packers
City
Green Bay, Wisconsin
Seating capacity
59,543
Playing surface
Grass
also
MILWAUKEE COUNTY STADIUM
City
Milwaukee, Wisconsin
Seating capacity
56,051
Playing serface
Grass

TEX-MEX CAESAR SALAD

2 heads romaine lettuce
1/2 cup olive oil
1 medium garlic clove, minced
36 corn tortilla triangles*

2-3 tomatoes, sliced
1/2 pound jicama, peeled, sliced julienne-style
1 avocado, cubed (optional)

DRESSING

3 medium garlic cloves, crushed
1/4 cup fresh lime juice
1 teaspoon anchovy paste
1/4 teaspoon black pepper

1 egg, coddled
1/2 cup olive oil
1/2 cup grated Parmesan cheese

(*Slice round tortillas into thirds.)

PRE-GAME:
Wash romaine; dry and tear into pieces.
Saute garlic in olive oil. Add tortilla triangles. Fry until crisp.
Drain on paper towels.

DRESSING: In large salad bowl, add garlic, lime juice,
anchovy paste and pepper. Whisk. Add egg, olive oil
and Parmesan cheese. Whisk after each addition.

HALF-TIME:
Dip avocado in lemon juice. Whisk dressing. Toss lettuce with tomatoes,
jicama, avocado and tortilla chips. Pour dressing over ingredients and toss
again

TEXAS STADIUM
Home team
Dallas Cowboys
City
Dallas, Texas
Seating capacity
65,024
Playing surface
Texas Turf

MOZZARELLA-MUSHROOM SALAD

1 medium head romaine lettuce
1 cucumber, peeled and cubed
1 avocado, pitted, peeled and cubed
1 stalk celery, sliced cross-wise
1/2 green pepper, thinly sliced
3-4 fresh mushrooms, thinly sliced
3/4 cup zesty Italian salad dressing
1 cup mozzarella cheese, shredded
Croutons

PRE-GAME:
Wash lettuce and pat dry. Tear into bite-size pieces.
Prepare vegetables and toss in large salad bowl. Refrigerate.

HALF-TIME:
Toss greens with salad dressing.
Add cheese and croutons. Toss again.

MILE-HIGH STADIUM
Home team
Denver Broncos
City
Denver, Colorado
Seating capacity
76,273
Playing surface
Grass

SPECIAL SPINACH SALAD

2 pounds fresh spinach
1 head iceberg lettuce

1/2 pound bacon, cooked, crumbled
1-1/2 cups large curd cottage cheese

DRESSING

1/4 cup sugar
1 teaspoon salt
1 teaspoon dry mustard
1 tablespoon onion juice

1/3 cup cider vinegar
1 cup salad oil
1 tablespoon poppy seeds

PRE-GAME:
Thoroughly wash and drain spinach; remove stems; break into bite-size pieces. Repeat with lettuce. Combine greens. Toss with bacon. Refrigerate.

DRESSING: Combine ingredients, except poppy seeds. Whisk. Add seeds. Mix again.

SECOND QUARTER:
Minutes before the **HALF**, mix dressing thoroughly and toss greens with half the dressing. Combine cottage cheese with remaining dressing, mix and toss with salad.

Yield: Serves 8-10

SUN DEVIL STADIUM
Home team
Phoenix Cardinals
City
Tempe, Arizona
Seating capacity
72,000
Playing surface
Grass

RED TIP LETTUCE SALAD WITH VERMOUTH DRESSING

1 head red tip lettuce
1/2 head romaine lettuce
1/2 head iceberg or Bibb lettuce
1-2 cucumbers, peeled, sliced
1/2 pint cherry tomatoes, halves
3 hard-boiled eggs
1 (7-ounce) jar pimiento-stuffed olives, drained, sliced
1/2 pound bacon, cooked, crumbled
2 (6-ounce) jars marinated artichoke hearts, drained, quartered
1/2 cup chopped green onions
1-1/2 cups croutons

VERMOUTH DRESSING

3/4 cup olive oil
3/4 cup salad oil
1/4 cup lemon juice
1/4 cup dry vermouth
2 teaspoons dry mustard
1 teaspoon pepper
1 clove garlic, crushed
1 teaspoon salt

PRE-GAME:
Tear greens into bite-size pieces.
Place all salad ingredients, except croutons, into large bowl and chill.

VERMOUTH DRESSING: Whisk oils with lemon juice and vermouth. Add remaining ingredients. Chill.

HALF-TIME:
Mix dressing. Toss with salad greens. Add croutons and toss again.

RICH STADIUM
Home team
Buffalo Bills
City
Orchard Park, New York
Seating capacity
80,290
Playing surface
AstroTurf

MONTEREY JACK MELANGE SALAD

1 head red leaf lettuce
1 head iceberg lettuce
1 cucumber, peeled, sliced, quartered
1/2-1 cup cherry tomatoes, halves

1/2 cup Parmesan cheese
   (or more), grated
3/4 cup Monterey Jack cheese
1-1/2 cups garlic croutons

DRESSING

1/4 cup oil
2 tablespoons apple cider vinegar
2 tablespoons Worcestershire sauce

2 teaspoons dried parsley flakes or
   2 tablespoons fresh parsley
1/4 teaspoon kosher salt

JACK MURPHY STADIUM
Home team
San Diego Chargers
City
San Diego, California
Seating capacity
60,750
Playing surface:
Grass

PRE-GAME:
Rinse and pat lettuce dry. Tear into pieces; cover and chill.
Prepare salad ingredients.
Pre-season salad bowl. (See p. 56)
Place salad ingredients in bowl, except cheese and croutons.
Refrigerate.

DRESSING: Whisk oil and vinegar together.
Add Worcestershire, parsley and salt, whisking after each addition.

HALF-TIME:
Whisk dressing. Toss with salad. Add croutons, Parmesan and Jack cheese. Toss again.

PASTA/SAUSAGE SALAD

1 package corkscrew, elbow macaroni or rotini (rainbow spirals)
1 teaspoon salt
1 cup red pepper, diced
1/3 cup green onions, thinly sliced
2-3 carrots, shedded
1/2 cup ripe olives, sliced
8 ounces hard salami, sliced
4 ounces pepperoni, thinly sliced
Italian dressing (optional)

DRESSING

1/3 cup mayonnaise
1/3 cup sour cream
1/3 cup milk
1/3 cup grated Parmesan cheese
1 clove garlic, minced
1/4 teaspoon salt
1/8 teaspoon cayenne pepper
Juice of 1 lemon (optional)

PRE-GAME:
Cook pasta in generous amount of boiling water with 1 tablespoon salt, stirring often. Drain and rinse with cold water.
Drain again and place in serving bowl.
Add red pepper, onion, carrots and olives; toss. Refrigerate covered.

DRESSING: In small bowl whisk mayonnaise, sour cream, milk, Parmesan, garlic, salt, pepper and lemon.

Mix pasta with dressing. Add salami and pepperoni, mixing well. Add Italian dressing to taste. Refrigerate several hours.

PONTIAC SILVERDOME
Home team:
Detroit Lions
City:
Pontiac, Michigan
Seating capacity:
80,500
Playing surface:
AstroTurf

PEAS AND CASHEW CRUNCH SALAD

2 (10-ounce) packages frozen peas
2 cups celery, diced
1/2 cup green onion, diced
2 cups salted cashew nuts, broken into small pieces
1/2 cup bacon, cooked, crumbled
1-1/2 cups sour cream
1/2 cup dressing

DRESSING

1-1/2 cups corn oil
1 teaspoon fresh lemon juice
1/2 cup red wine vinegar
1/2 tablespoon Worcestershire sauce
1/2 teaspoon salt
1/2 teaspoon ground pepper
1/2 teaspoon Dijon mustard
1/2 clove garlic, minced
1/2 teaspoon sugar

PRE-GAME:
Mix all salad ingredients except peas. Add dressing and toss. Add peas and toss.

DRESSING: Whisk corn oil with lemon juice and wine vinegar. Mix with remaining ingredients. Yield: 1 pint.

HALF-TIME:
Mound salad atop lettuce leaves.

Note: Dressing works well on other salads and vegetables.

KINGDOME
Home team
Seattle Seahawks
City
Seattle, Washington
Seating capacity
64,984
Playing surface
AstroTurf

SOUR CREAM POTATO SALAD

- 5 cups diced, boiled potatoes
- 1 tablespoon onion, grated
- 1/2 cup cucumber, diced
- 1/2 teaspoon celery seed
- 1-1/2 teaspoons salt
- 1/2 teaspoon ground pepper
- 2 tablespoons fresh parsley, chopped
- 2 stalks celery, sliced approximately 1/8" thick
- 2-3 green onions, with 2" green tops, sliced
- 1 (2-ounce) jar pimiento
- 4 hard-boiled eggs,
- 1-1/2 cups sour cream
- 1/2 cup mayonnaise
- 1/4 cup balsamic or apple cider vinegar
- 2 teaspoons prepared mustard

PRE-GAME:
Cook potatoes in their skins. Peel. While still warm combine and mix with onion, cucumber, celery seed, salt, pepper, parsley, celery, green onions and pimiento. Add 3 diced egg whites. Combine 3 mashed egg yolks with sour cream, mayonnaise, vinegar and mustard. Add to potatoes and blend gently. Refrigerate several hours.
Salt and pepper to taste.
Garnish with one or more sliced eggs.

Yield: 10 servings

Note: A good quality California white potato boiled in its skin makes an excellent potato for salads.

SOLDIER FIELD
Home team
Chicago Bears
City
Chicago, Illinios
Seating capacity
66,946
Playing surface
Grass

COBB SALAD

1/2 head iceberg lettuce, finely chopped
1/2 bunch watercress, chopped
1 small bunch chicory, finely chopped
2-1/2 tablespoons fresh chives, minced
3 small tomatoes, peeled, seeded, chopped

2-1/2 cups cooked chicken breasts, diced
8 slices bacon, cooked, crumbled
3 hard-boiled eggs, finely diced
3 ounces blue cheese, crumbled
1-2 avocados, pitted, peeled and diced

COBB DRESSING

1/3 cup olive oil
1 cup salad oil
1/3 cup red wine vinegar
1 teaspoon lemon juice
1/3 cup water
1/4 teaspoon sugar

2 teaspoons salt
1 teaspoon freshly ground pepper
1 teaspoon Worcestershire sauce
1/4 teaspoon dry mustard
1/2 clove garlic, minced

FIRST-QUARTER:
Prepare greens and remaining salad ingredients. Refrigerate.

DRESSING: Whisk oils with vinegar and lemon juice. Add remaining ingredients and whisk. Store in refrigerator.

HALF-TIME:
Mix salad ingredients with 3/4 cup dressing. Add more if needed.

Yield: 5 servings

R F K STADIUM
Home team
Washington Redskins
City
Washington D.C.
Seating Capacity
55,672
Playing surface
Grass

ROMAINE SALAD AND BLUE CHEESE DRESSING

2 heads romaine lettuce,
1 hard-boiled egg, chopped
1 (2-ounce) package slivered almonds, browned
3/4 cup garlic-flavored croutons

DRESSING

1-1/2 teaspoons red wine vinegar
1 clove garlic, minced
1/8 teaspoon dry mustard
1/4 teaspoon freshly ground pepper
1/4 teaspoon onion powder
1/4 teaspoon Worcestershire sauce
Pinch cayenne pepper
2 tablespoons sour cream
1 cup mayonnaise
1/4 cup buttermilk
1/2 cup blue cheese, crumbled

PRE-GAME:
Rinse and pat lettuce dry. Tear into bite-size pieces; cover and chill. Toast almonds in 350-degree oven until brown.

DRESSING: Whisk vinegar, garlic, mustard, pepper, onion powder, Worcestershire sauce and cayenne pepper together. Combine sour cream and mayonnaise. Thin with buttermilk. Mix with whisked ingredients. Add 1/4 cup blue cheese. Refrigerate overnight.

HALF-TIME:
Toss dressing and romaine together. Garnish with chopped egg, almonds, croutons and remaining blue cheese.

RIVERFRONT STADIUM
Home Team
Cincinnati Bengals
City
Cincinnati, Ohio
Seating capacity
59,755
Playing surface
AstroTurf-8

"THREE R" ROMAINE, RAISIN AND RED DRESSING SALAD

1 large head romaine lettuce
1/2 cup slivered almonds
1/2 cup golden raisins

6-8 bacon slices, cooked, crumbled
1 medium avocado
Salt and pepper

DRESSING

1/4 cup salad oil
2 tablespoons red wine vinegar
3 tablespoons ketchup

1 tablespoon soy sauce
1 tablespoon sugar

PRE-GAME:
Spread almonds in shallow pan and toast in 350-degree oven until golden brown, about 8 minutes. Set aside.
Cook bacon; set aside.
Rinse and pat lettuce dry. Tear into bite-size pieces; cover and chill.

DRESSING: Whisk oil and vinegar. Add ketchup, soy sauce and sugar. Whisk after each addition. Store in a jar. Refrigerate.

HALF-TIME:
Combine romaine, almonds, raisins and bacon; add dressing.
Season with salt and pepper to taste.
Peel and slice avocado (dip in lemon juice, if necessary). Arrange on top.

Yield: 5-6 servings

THREE RIVERS STADIUM
Home team
Pittsburgh Steelers
City
Pittsburgh, Pennsylvania
Seating capacity
59,000
Playing surface
AstroTurf

TOMATO, SHRIMP AND AVOCADO SALAD

3 heads Bibb lettuce
1-1/2 pounds shrimp, peeled, cleaned
15 cherry tomatoes, sliced
10 slices bacon, cooked, crumbled
3/4 cup Monterey Jack cheese, shredded
1 avocado
Salt and pepper

CREAMY AVOCADO DRESSING

1/2 cup buttermilk
1 (3-ounce) package cream cheese, softened
Juice of 1 lemon
1 clove garlic, minced
1/4 teaspoon salt
1/4 teaspoon hot pepper sauce
1 medium avocado, pitted, peeled, chopped

PRE-GAME:
Wash lettuce and pat dry. Tear into bite-size pieces.
Toss salad ingredients except lettuce and avocado. Refrigerate.

DRESSING: Blend all ingredients. Refrigerate.

SECOND QUARTER:
Dip avocado in lemon juice. Slice or cube.

HALF-TIME:
Toss salad ingredients with dressing

TAMPA STADIUM
Home team
Tampa Bay Buccaneers
City
Tampa Bay, Flordia
Seating capacity
74,315
Playing surface
Grass

THE FOOTBALL FIELD

OFFENSE

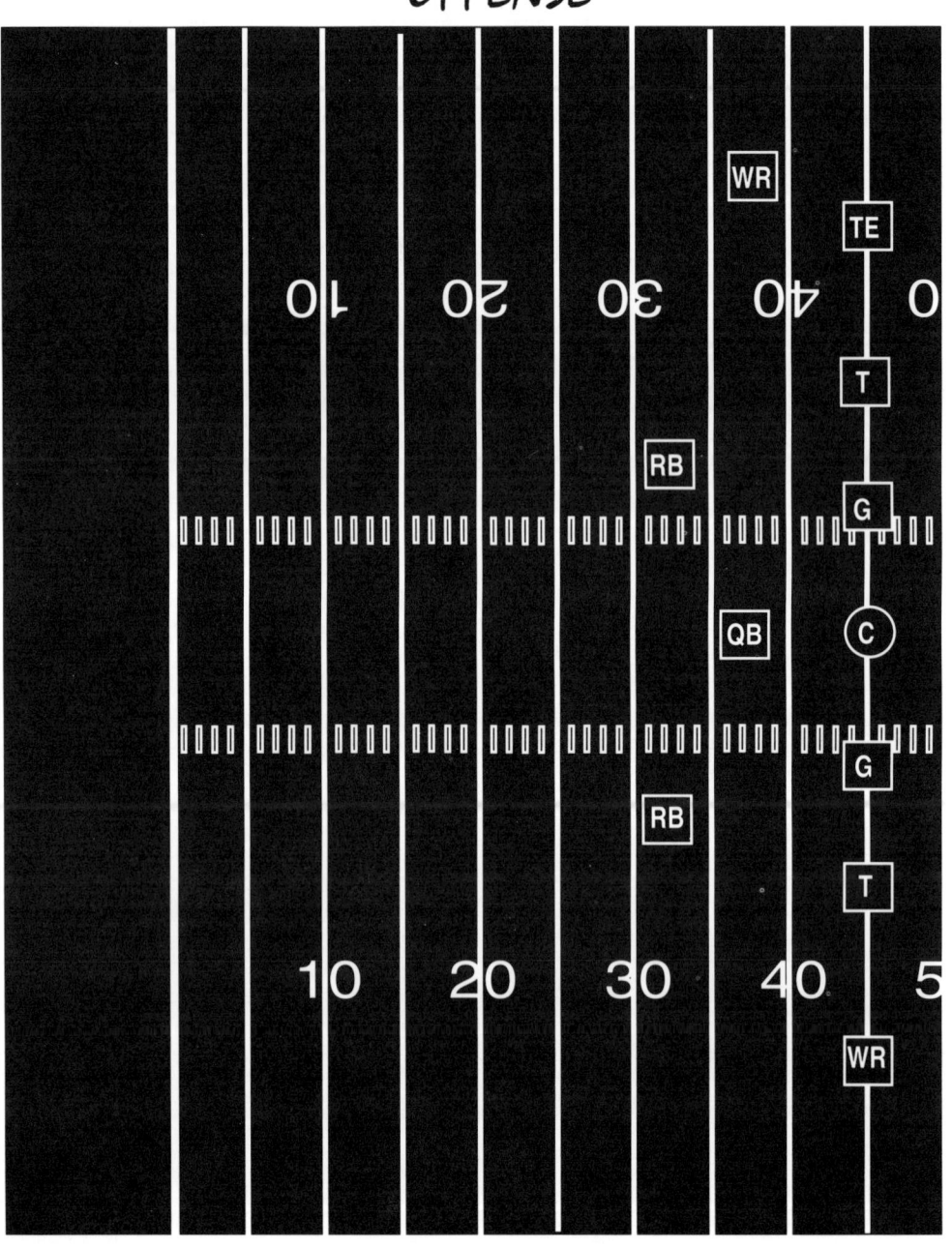

TE	TIGHT END
T	TACKLE
G	GUARD
C	CENTER

WR	WIDE RECEIVER
RB	RUNNING BACK
QB	QUARTERBACK

76

DEFENSE

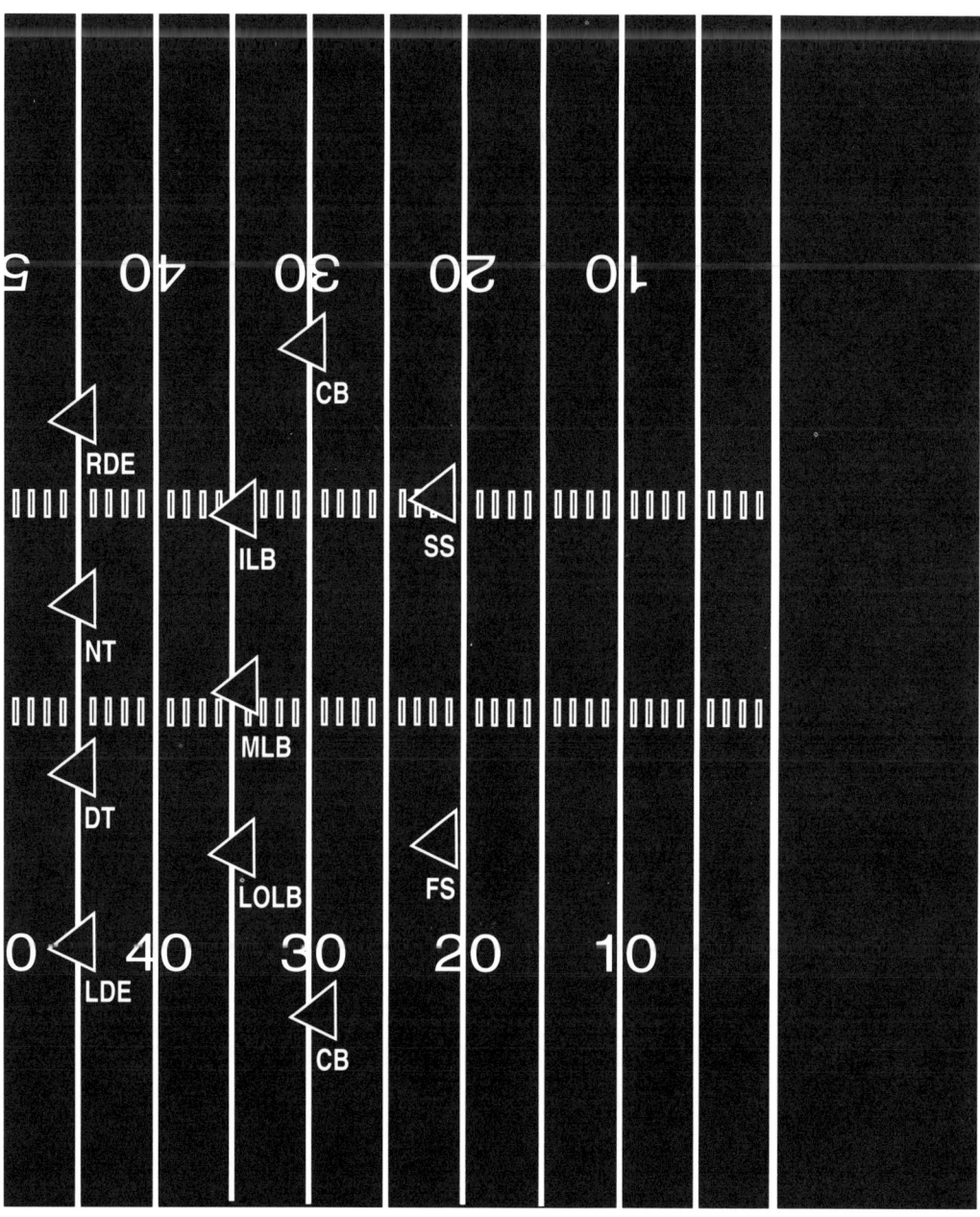

RDE	RIGHT DEFENSIVE END
NT	NOSE TACKLE
DT	DEFENSIVE TACKLE
LDE	LEFT DEFENSIVE END
ILB	INSIDE LINEBACKER
MLB	MIDDLE LINEBACKER
LOLB	LEFT OUTSIDE LINEBACKER
CB	CORNERBACK
SS	STRONG SAFETY
FS	FREE SAFETY

ENTREES
OFFENSIVE AND DEFENSIVE POSITIONS

Novices to football always ask, "Who has the ball?" Hopefully, this section will help answer that question.

The principal ingredient of most entrees is meat, fish or poultry. In football, the focus is the offense and defense. Consequently, the fish and chicken recipes will represent the lighter, offensive positions. The "beefy" defensive positions will be discussed in the meat entrees. Knowing these positions will help in tracking the ball.

Football again serves as a backdrop to tasty dishes ranging from a spicy meatloaf to a lemon-flavored swordfish and exotic fruit salsa.

Bring on the starting line-up positions or the entrees.

OFFENSIVE LINE
(Offensive Players' Onion Soup)

X **WIDE RECEIVER**
(Wide Receivers Wild Rice and Chicken Vol-Au-Vent)

X **FLANKER**
(Flanker Swordfish Shish-Kabob and Aloha Salsa)

X **TACKLE**
(Tackle Teriyaki Salmon)

X **RUNNING BACK**
(Fullback Chicken Florentine)

X **GUARD**
(Guard au Gratin Baked Fish)

X **CENTER**
(Center Cheese Chowder)

X **QUARTERBACK**
(Quarterback Grilled or Barbequed Chicken)

X **GUARD**
(Guard the Pocket Sandwiches)

X **RUNNING BACK**
(Halfback Halibut)

X **TACKLE**
(Tackle Fractured Turkey Tacos)

X **TIGHT END**
(Tight End Chiladas—Chicken)

OFFENSIVE PLAYERS ONION SOUP

4 tablespoons butter or margarine
4 tablespoons oil
10 large yellow onions
Salt and pepper to taste
16 cups (4 quarts) beef broth
Swiss cheese, grated
Baguette French Bread, sliced

PRE-GAME:
Slice onions and place in large pot or Dutch oven with oil and margarine; cook approximately 15 minutes. When onions are translucent, add salt, pepper and broth. (Canned broth is stronger. When using your own broth, add bouillon cubes or powder.) Bring ingredients to a boil, reduce to simmer. Cook 40 minutes.
Use baguettes to make croutons. Season with garlic.
See Crew-tons (croutons) page 159.

FIRST QUARTER:
Heat soup on low.

HALF-TIME:
Place small amount of grated Swiss cheese on the bottom of each bowl or cup. Add soup and top with 1 or more crouton slices. Add additional cheese.

Yield: 12-14 servings

The attack or offensive team must attempt to advance the ball on four downs. The following starting positions constitute the offensive line and backfield: tight end, tackles, guards, center, wide receivers, running backs (halfback and fullback) and quarterback.

FLANKER SWORDFISH SHISH KABOB AND ALOHA SALSA

3 pounds swordfish, cut into 1-inch chunks

MARINADE

- 3/4 cup fresh lemon juice
- 1/2 cup olive oil
- 1 clove garlic, finely minced
- 1 onion, cut into rings
- 2 bay leaves
- Salt and pepper

SKEWERED VEGETABLES

- 3 bell peppers—one each, red, green and yellow
- 1 medium yellow onion, cut into 1-1/2" pieces
- Cherry tomatoes

ALOHA SALSA

- 1 cup pineapple, peeled, diced
- 1 cup papaya, peeled, diced
- 1 cup mango, peeled, diced
- 2 tomatoes, skinned, seeded, diced
- 1/3 cup green onion, chopped
- 3 tablespoons fresh cilantro, chopped
- 1 small jalapeño chili, minced
- 1-1/2 tablespoons fresh lime juice
- Pinch salt

A football program might designate this offensive player a wide receiver. He can also be called the flanker if he's positioned two yards behind the line of scrimmage and six to eight yards outside the tight end.

PRE-GAME:

MARINADE: Whisk lemon juice and oil together in small bowl. Add garlic, onion and bay leaves. Season with salt and pepper. Place swordfish in shallow dish and cover with marinade. Cover. Refrigerate 6 or more hours. Prepare vegetable skewers.

SALSA: Toss all ingredients together gently. Marinate at least 6 hours in refrigerator. Salsa should be served at room temperature.

SECOND QUARTER:

Thread swordfish onto skewers. Prepare charcoal for grilling early in quarter. Place skewers and vegetables on own or separate skewers on grill 5-10 minutes before end of quarter. Turn after 6-7 minutes and baste swordfish with marinade. (You may wish to place tomatoes on their own skewers since they grill more quickly than peppers and onions.)

Yield: 6-7 servings

TACKLE TERIYAKI SALMON

6 or more salmon fillets, skinned and cut into serving-size pieces

MARINADE

1 bottle Teriyaki sauce
Equal amount of water

1 clove garlic, minced
1/2 teaspoon fresh ginger, minced

BUTTER SAUCE

1 cube margarine
Juice of 1 lemon

1/2 teaspoon fresh dill, minced
1 tablespoon fresh parsley, minced

> *Two tackles line up between the guards and the ends (tight end and wide receiver). Offensive tackles block the defensive linemen, open up holes for runners up the middle and try to protect the quarterback.*

PRE-GAME:
Place marinade ingredients in a plastic lock-top bag with salmon pieces. Marinate 1 hour. Remove salmon; pat dry with paper towels.
In separate dish, add lemon juice, dill and parsley to melted margarine.

SECOND QUARTER:
Place fish on heated barbecue grill. Do not overcook. Allow approximately 10 minutes cooking time per 1" thickness of fish.
Grill fish, dip in melted butter sauce and place on warmed platter.

Variation:
6 salmon fillets, skinned and cut in serving-size pieces
1 bottle teriyaki sauce
Equal amount of water
1 cube margarine
1 handful of green onions, chopped

Marinate salmon in teriyaki sauce and water.
Melt margarine and onions together.
Remove salmon and pat dry with paper towels.
Grill fish. When almost cooked, remove from grill and lay in onion/margarine mixture. Return to grill until done; place on a warmed platter.

GUARD
AU GRATIN BAKED FISH

3 pounds fillet of sole
8 slices sharp cheddar cheese
1 teaspoon thyme or oregano
1/4 cup or more fresh parsley, chopped
1 cup onions, chopped

2 tablespoons olive oil
2 tablespoons flour
1 teaspoon salt
1/8 teaspoon pepper
1 cup milk

PRE-GAME:
Place half the fillets in a greased 9" x 9" x 1-3/4" pan.
Cover with 4 slices of cheese.
Top with another layer of fillets and cheese.
Sprinkle with thyme and parsley.
Saute onions in oil over medium heat until clear and lightly browned.
Blend in flour, salt and pepper. Slowly stir in milk; bring to boil over low heat, stirring constantly. Boil approximately 1 minute until thick.
Pour over fish.

SECOND QUARTER:
Bake 20-30 minutes in pre-heated 400-degree oven.

Yield: 6-8 servings

Note: Some white fish can be fairly bland, but this recipe makes most white fish taste great. Those not fond of fish may be converted after trying this dish.

Two guards are on the line of scrimmage opposite the center. They try to block the defensive linemen to protect the quarterback. Guards create the holes in the line for runs up the middle. Offensive guards may not always get the glory, but a strong offensive line sure makes the quarterback look good.

CENTER CHEESE CHOWDER

3/4 pound zucchini, sliced (approximately 4 small ones)
2 small onions, sliced
1 (16-ounce) can garbanzo beans, drained
1 (16-ounce) can diced tomatoes, undrained
1/2 cup margarine
1-1/2 cups dry white wine
2 teaspoons salt
1/4 teaspoon pepper
2 teaspoons fresh garlic, minced
1 teaspoon basil
1 bay leaf
1 cup Monterey Jack cheese, shredded
1 cup grated Parmesan cheese
1 cup whipping cream
3/4 pound medium shrimp, shelled and boiled or
3/4 pound crabmeat

The center puts the ball in play from the line of scrimmage. He snaps the ball, usually to the quarterback or kicker.

PRE-GAME:
Combine first 11 ingredients in 3-quart baking dish. Cover. Bake at 400 degrees for 1 hour, stirring after half hour. Stir in cheese, followed by cream and finally seafood. Cover. Bake 10 minutes longer.

SECOND QUARTER:
Reheat, making sure soup doesn't burn.

Note: This can be made a day ahead. Just combine the first 11 ingredients and bake for one hour. Cool. Refrigerate overnight. Bring back to temperature (bubbling) and then add cheese, cream and seafood. Bake for an additional 10 minutes.

GUARD THE POCKET SANDWICHES

8 whole wheat pita pocket rounds
1 (3-4 pound) cooked chicken, shredded
3 carrots, grated
3 stalks celery, sliced
1/2 head lettuce, thinly sliced
2 cups whole kernel corn, fresh, frozen and defrosted or canned

Cherry tomatoes, sliced in half
1 bunch green onions, thinly sliced
Alfalfa sprouts
2 avocados, diced
2 cups pineapple cubes, fresh or canned
1 red or green pepper, thinly sliced (optional)
Button mushrooms, thinly sliced (optional)

PRE-GAME:
Slice pita rounds in half.
Prepare remaining ingredients. Place in separate bowls. Refrigerate.

SECOND-QUARTER:
Set out pita rounds and bowls of chicken, vegetables and fruit.

HALF-TIME:
Fans may prepare their sandwiches buffet-style.

The quarterback needs a protected pocket from which to throw. The guard is one of seven offensive players required to be set on the line of scrimmage before the play. He helps protect the passer.

TACKLE
FRACTURED TURKEY TACOS

1-1/2 pounds cooked turkey, shredded
1 teaspoon olive oil
1 large onion, chopped
2 cloves garlic, minced
1 teaspoon chili powder
1/2 teaspoon ground cumin
1 teaspoon oregano
1 teaspoon salt
1 (6-ounce) can chopped green chiles (optional)
1 (6-ounce) can tomato paste
1 (8-ounce) can tomato sauce
1-1/2 cups water
1-1/2 cups cooked rice
1 (10-ounce) bag corn chips
1/2 head lettuce
2 tomatoes, chopped
2 avocados, diced
2 cups cheddar cheese, shredded
Hot sauce or salsa

PRE-GAME:
Saute onion in olive oil until limp. Add turkey, garlic, chili powder, cumin, oregano, salt and chiles; cook 5 minutes.
Add tomato paste, tomato sauce and water; simmer 25-30 minutes.

SECOND QUARTER:
Just before serving, add cooked rice to sauce.

HALF-TIME:
On a platter, layer corn chips first, followed by tomato sauce, lettuce, tomatoes, avocado and top with cheese. Sprinkle with hot sauce or salsa.

Yield: 6 servings

Note: 1-1/2 pounds cooked ground beef may be substituted for turkey.

Tackles are members of the offensive line positioned between the guards and ends. Tackles try to prevent the defensive ends from reaching the quarterback.

TIGHT END CHILADAS—CHICKEN

1 large onion, chopped
2 tablespoons olive oil
1 garlic clove, minced
2 cups tomato puree
2 cans chopped green chiles
2 cups cooked chicken, shredded
Salt and pepper

12 corn tortillas
6 teaspoons chicken bouillon powder
3 cups cream (or 1/2 cup milk, 1/2 cup sour cream)
1/2 pound Monterey Jack cheese
4 green onions, sliced
Garnish: (optional) avocado slices, green olives, chopped hard-boiled eggs

PRE-GAME:
Saute chopped onion in olive oil until soft. Add garlic, puree, chiles and chicken.
Season with salt and pepper to taste; simmer 10 minutes.
Fry tortillas lightly in approximately 1" oil.
Dissolve bouillon in hot cream or milk/sour cream mixture.
Dip each tortilla in cream and fill with chicken mixture.
Roll filled tortillas and arrange in 9" x 13" pan.
Pour remaining cream mixture over enchiladas.
Top with Jack cheese. Refrigerate.

FIRST QUARTER:
End of quarter bake in 350-degree oven for 30 minutes.

SECOND QUARTER:
Remove from oven. Garnish green onions, avocados, green olives or eggs.

Yield: 6 servings, 2 enchiladas each

There's usually only one tight end on the line of scrimmage. He's positioned next to a guard. On a running play this end will help the offensive linemen by blocking. Tight ends are usually big and quick which enables them to not only block but handle running short pass patterns. Their jerseys sport numbers 80-89.

WIDE RECEIVERS WILD RICE AND CHICKEN VOL-AU-VENT

6 chicken thighs	1 cup light cream
2 tablespoons margarine	1 (6-ounce) can sliced mushrooms, drained
1 teaspoon powdered chicken bouillon	
1/2 cup hot water	1/4 cup dry white wine
3 tablespoons flour	6 sausages, cooked
1/4 teaspoon salt	1 (10-ounce) package frozen patty shells, thawed
1/4 teaspoon paprika	
Dash pepper	2 cups wild rice, cooked
	2 cups brown rice, cooked

PRE-GAME:

Brown chicken in margarine.
Dissolve bouillon in water, add to chicken, cover, simmer 30 minutes.
Remove chicken, cool and remove bone.
Add enough water to pan to make 1 cup of broth.
Combine flour, seasonings and cream. When well mixed, add to broth.
Heat until thick and bubbly, stirring constantly to avoid a lumpy sauce.
Add mushrooms and wine.
Place cooked sausage in each bone cavity.
Roll out pastry and place thigh on each shell, top with 2 tablespoons sauce.
Fold pastry, seal seams and fold ends.

SECOND QUARTER:

Bake thighs at 400 degrees for 30 minutes. Heat extra sauce and serve with the thighs and wild rice.

Yield: 6 servings

Wide receivers can be set more than six yards from their tight ends or on the ends of the line of scrimmage. These strong and agile players are characterized by speed and/or the ability to catch the ball. Flankers and split ends are considered wide receivers.

FULLBACK CHICKEN FLORENTINE

3-1/2 to 4 pounds chicken breasts
2 boxes chopped spinach, thawed
1 (8-ounce) carton ricotta cheese
1 (3-ounce) package cream cheese
3 ounces Parmesan cheese
1 clove garlic, minced
3 tablespoons chopped onion
2 tablespoons parsley
Juice of 1/2 lemon
1 tablespoon Worcestershire sauce

PRE-GAME:
Clean chicken breasts.
Drain spinach thoroughly and mix with remaining ingredients.
Lift skin of chicken breast enough to form a pocket, leaving skin partially attached. Tuck spinach mixture under the skin. Pull skin over filling.
Place in greased baking dish.

FIRST-QUARTER:
Place covered dish in oven at end of *Quarter*.
Bake for 25 minutes at 350 degrees.
Remove cover and bake 5-10 until golden brown.

Fullbacks can be counted on for runs into the line, blocking or handling pass plays. Set four yards behind the quarterback these offensive backfield players are used on short yardage situations.

HALF BACK HALIBUT

3 pounds halibut
Dry white wine
Seasoned bread crumbs
2 cups sour cream
1 cup mayonnaise
1 cup onion, finely chopped (optional)
Paprika

PRE-GAME:
Cut halibut into serving-size pieces. Place in bowl and marinate in white wine 2 hours. Drain and pat pieces dry.
Roll in fine bread crumbs.
Place coated pieces in single layer in baking dish.
Mix sour cream, mayonnaise and onions.
Spread sauce over fish, smoothing to edges of dish.
Sprinkle with additional bread crumbs and paprika.

SECOND QUARTER:
Bake at 500 degrees 15-20 minutes until light, brown and bubbly. Don't overcook halibut or it becomes dry.

Yield: 6-8 servings

Note: Another version for halibut
　　　1 cube margarine
　　　1 yellow onion, sliced
　　　Mayonnaise
　　　Seasoned bread crumbs

Melt margarine in baking pan with sliced onion. Heat in 350-degree oven until onion becomes soft. Place halibut pieces on top. Coat halibut with mayonnaise about 1/4" thick. Top with seasoned bread crumbs. Bake according to above directions. Generally, you need to cook fish 10 minutes for each inch of thickness.

Today the term running back is widely used. Both halibut and half-backs are elusive sprinters, preferring not to be caught. When the quarterback hands off the ball to the speedy running back, look for him to take off down field eluding the catch of any tackles.

QUARTERBACK GRILLED OR BARBECUED CHICKEN

2 tablespoons margarine
1 tablespoon dry mustard
1/2 cup maple syrup
1 cup chili sauce
1/2 cup ketchup
1/2 cup apple cider vinegar
1 teaspoon celery seed
1/2 teaspoon salt
1 teaspoon cayenne pepper
1/2 teaspoon black pepper
2 (3-pound) chickens, cut into serving pieces
Olive oil for grill

PRE-GAME:
Melt margarine. Add all ingredients, except chicken.
Heat mixture to boiling, reduce to simmer for 20 minutes, uncovered.
Cool.
Place chicken in 1 or 2 large dishes or pans.
Toss pieces with sauce to coat lightly. Reserve remaining sauce for basting.
Refrigerate, covered, overnight.

FIRST QUARTER:
Before fans arrive, remove chicken from refrigerator. Pat dry.
If cooking over coals, preheat grill. Brush rack with oil.
Cook with vents open for 15 minutes on each side. Remove cover; baste with sauce and continue cooking 5 minutes on each side.

SECOND QUARTER:
May also be broiled 20 minutes each side in oven if barbeque is unavailable.
Reheat remaining sauce to serve on the side.

The quarterback position is usually the glamorous job—except when he's getting grilled or barbecued by the defense. The "QB" lines up behind the center and is usually responsible for play-calling. The designated offensive players try to place the quarterback in a protected position or pocket. Quarterback's jerseys are numbered 1-19.

DEFENSIVE LINE
(Defensive Formation Beef Stroganoff)

    X **CORNERBACK**
       (Cornerback Chili)

X **DEFENSIVE END**
  (Beefy Defensive End Chiladas)

      X **SAFETY**
        (Savory Vegetable Soup)

    X **LINEBACKER**
     (Linebacker Basil Burgers)

X **DEFENSIVE TACKLE**
  (Defensive Tackle Tamale Pie)

     X **LINEBACKER**
      (Sack the QB Salsa and Beef Fajitas)

X **DEFENSIVE TACKLE**
  (Defensive Linemen Lasagna)

      X **SAFETY**
       (Free-Safety Seasoned Meatloaf)

X **DEFENSIVE END**
  (Roughing the Kicker Kabobs)

     X **LINEBACKER**
      (Rushing the Passer Roast Beef Pasta)

      X **CORNERBACK**
       (Defensive Back Beef Bourguignon)

DEFENSIVE FORMATION BEEF STROGANOFF

1 pound fresh mushrooms
1 stick margarine
2 tablespoons parsley
1/2 teaspoon garlic salt
1/4 teaspoon pepper
1 pound sirloin, sliced in strips
1 (16-ounce) carton sour cream or imitation sour cream
1-1/4 cups sauterne wine
1/4 teaspoon seasoned pepper
2 tablespoons flour
3 green onions, chopped
Cooked rice or noodles

PRE-GAME:

Slice mushrooms and saute in margarine. Add parsley, garlic salt and pepper. Remove mushrooms from pan and saute meat strips or cubes. Brown on all sides and remove.
In same pan dilute sour cream or its imitation with 1 cup sauterne.
In separate bowl mix 1/4 cup sauterne, seasoned pepper and flour thoroughly. Add to pan mixture.
(If sauce becomes too thick use more wine to dilute.)
Add green onions.

SECOND QUARTER:

Cook rice or noodles.
Reheat stroganoff until hot, but do not let it boil.

HALF TIME:

Serve with rice or noodles.

The team that does not have the ball is referred to as the defense. The 11 players, in the 4-3 formation, consist of 4 linemen, 3 linebackers, 2 cornerbacks and 2 safeties.

BEEFY DEFENSIVE END CHILADAS

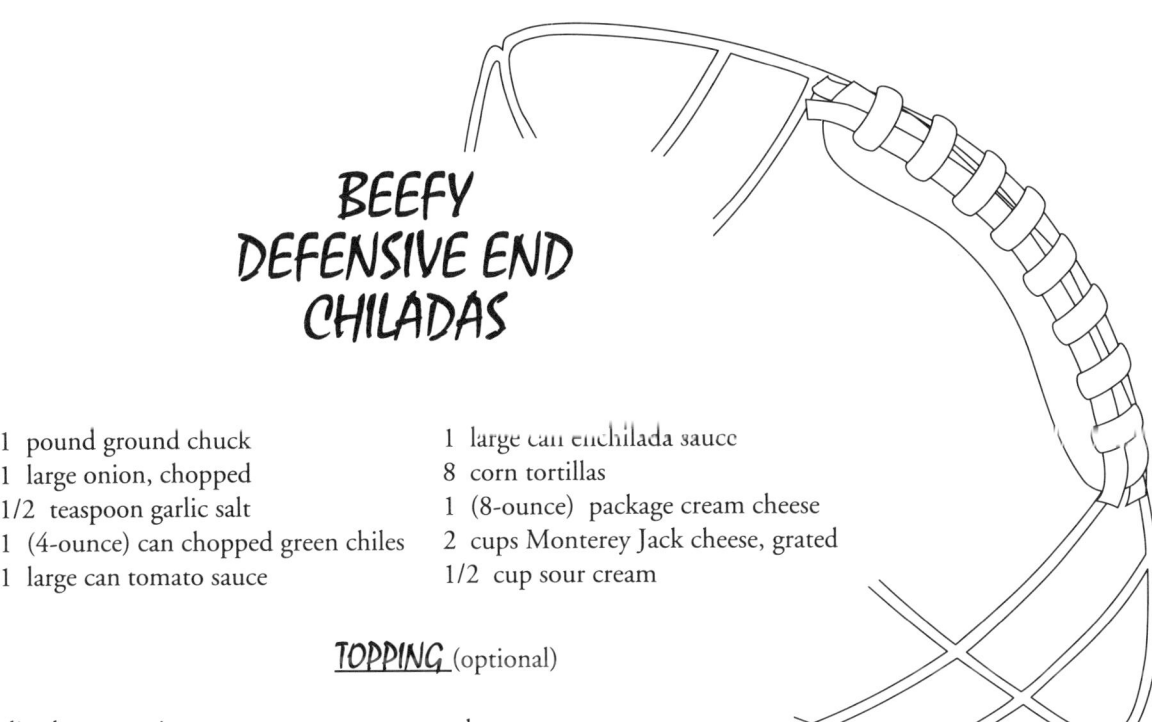

1 pound ground chuck
1 large onion, chopped
1/2 teaspoon garlic salt
1 (4-ounce) can chopped green chiles
1 large can tomato sauce
1 large can enchilada sauce
8 corn tortillas
1 (8-ounce) package cream cheese
2 cups Monterey Jack cheese, grated
1/2 cup sour cream

TOPPING (optional)

sliced green onions
sliced black olives
salsa
guacamole

PRE-GAME:
Brown meat in olive oil. Add onion and cook until soft.
Drain and return to pan. Sprinkle with garlic salt. Add chiles, tomato sauce and enchilada sauce; simmer 30 minutes.
Spread bottom of a 9" x 13" pan evenly with some sauce.
Soften corn tortillas in pan with a little olive oil for a few seconds. Drain on paper towels. Slice cream cheese lengthwise into 8 pieces.
Place slice of cream cheese and meat mixture inside each tortilla and roll up.
Place in rectangular pan. Top with remaining meat sauce.
Sprinkle Monterey Jack cheese over casserole.
Cover with foil.

FIRST QUARTER:
Bake at 350 degrees for 45 minutes.

HALF-TIME:
Serve with a dollop of sour cream.
Optional: Top with sliced green onions, black olives, salsa and guacamole.

There are right and left defensive ends on the line of scrimmage outside the tackles. They are usually lighter and quicker than the tackles. Their primary purpose is to damage the quarterback's effectiveness.

DEFENSIVE TACKLE TAMALE PIE

2 pounds ground beef
2 packages chili mix
1 (6-ounce) can whole kernel corn
1 (16-ounce) can tomato sauce
1 cup cheddar cheese, shredded
1 can pitted whole olives
8 ounces corn meal
2 cups water

PRE-GAME:
Saute beef in small amount of olive oil, drain off fat.
Combine beef, chili mix, corn, tomato sauce, cheese and olives in baking dish.
Mix corn meal and water. Spread over the meat mixture.

SECOND QUARTER:
Bake pie in preheated 400-degree oven 35 minutes.

Yield: 8 servings

The two defensive tackles are the heavyweights on the field. They try to stop any run through the middle of the line. The defensive tackle opposite the center is often referred to as the "nose tackle". A defensive player once said this position was like "being the fire hydrant at a dog show."

DEFENSIVE LINEMEN LASAGNA

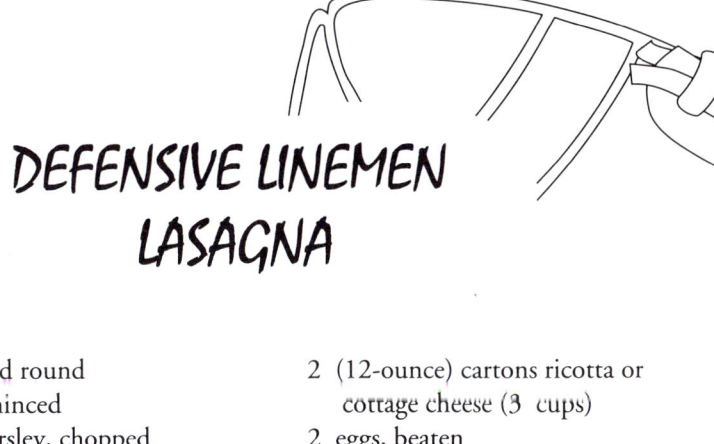

2 pounds ground round
1 clove garlic, minced
1 tablespoon parsley, chopped
1 tablespoon basil
1-1/2 teaspoon salt
1 (1-pound) can tomatoes
2 (6-ounce) cans tomato paste
1 (10-ounce) package lasagna noodles

2 (12-ounce) cartons ricotta or cottage cheese (3 cups)
2 eggs, beaten
2 teaspoons salt
1/2 teaspoon pepper
2 tablespoons chopped parsley
1/2 cup grated Parmesan cheese
3 packages mozzarella cheese, thinly sliced

PRE-GAME:

Brown meat slowly, spoon off excess fat. Add garlic, parsley, basil, salt, tomatoes and tomato paste to meat mixture. Simmer uncovered until thick, 45 minutes to 1 hour, stirring occasionally.
Cook noodles in boiling salted water until tender; drain, rinse in cold water. Combine cheese with eggs, salt, pepper, parsley and Parmesan cheese.
Place half the noodles in a 13" x 9" x 2" baking dish.
Spread half the cottage cheese mixture over noodles; add half the mozzarella cheese and half the meat mixture. Repeat layers.

FIRST QUARTER:

Bake in a moderate oven at 375 degrees for 30 minutes. Let stand 10-15 minutes before cutting in squares. Cover with foil and keep warm in a 200-degree oven until *Half-Time*.

Defensive linemen are the front four men on the line of scrimmage, in the popular 4-3 lineup (4 linemen, 3 linebackers). The two inside linemen are defensive tackles and the outside linemen are called defensive ends.

ROUGHING THE KICKER KABOBS

Use approximately 1/2 pound of lean beef sirloin for each person or you may wish to use the same amount of lamb. You or the butcher may cut the meat into 1-1/2" to 2" cubes. If using lamb, ask for either the leg or the shoulder with most of the fat removed.

MARINADE

1/2 cup salad oil
1/4 cup tarragon vinegar
3 tablespoons lemon juice
2 tablespoon prepared mustard
2 tablespoons soy sauce

1/2 teaspoon salt
1 teaspoon garlic salt
1/4 teaspoon freshly ground pepper
1 bay leaf
1 medium onion, sliced and separated

SKEWERED VEGETABLES

Whole cherry tomatoes
Mushroom caps
Yellow onions, cut in 1-1/2 to 2" pieces

Green peppers, cut in 1-1/2" pieces
Optional: eggplant, zucchini

This penalty is called when a defensive player runs into the kicker in a violent manner. It results in a fifteen-yard penalty plus an automatic first down. Defensive ends rush the passer or kicker.

PRE-GAME:
Slice beef or lamb into cubes.
MARINADE: Mix ingredients. Marinate meat overnight.
Arrange cubes of meat on skewers alternating with vegetables.
(Place tomatoes on separate skewers. They cook very quickly.)

SECOND QUARTER:
The gas grill or briquets should be ready 15 minutes before *Half-Time*.
Grill approximately 10-20 minutes.
(Grilling time depends on size of cubes.)

HALF-TIME:
Remove from skewers onto heated platter.

LINEBACKER BASIL BURGERS

- 1 pound ground beef
- 1 pound ground turkey
- 1 egg, slightly beaten
- 2/3 cup onion, chopped
- 1/2 cup grated Parmesan cheese
- 1/4 cup fresh basil, snipped
- 1/4 cup ketchup
- 2 cloves garlic, minced
- 1/4 teaspoon salt
- 1/4 teaspoon pepper

PRE-GAME:
In large mixing bowl combine egg, onion, Parmesan cheese, basil, ketchup, garlic, salt and pepper. Add ground beef and turkey; mix well. Shape into 8 patties.

SECOND QUARTER:
Midway through the quarter place patties on grill. Grill over medium coals for 15-18 minutes or until juices run clear, turning once.

Serve with hamburger buns, tomatoes, pickles, cheese slices, grilled or raw onions, lettuce, seasoned mushrooms, mayonnaise, mustard, relish and ketchup. To make seasoned mushrooms, saute sliced mushrooms in margarine. Add Italian seasoning and rosemary to taste.

Yield: 8 servings

Note: Make burgers ahead of time. Place uncooked patties in freezer wrap and freeze up to 3 months. The night before grilling, remove from freezer.

The three linebackers are behind the linemen. They may be referred to as weak or strong-side linebackers or inside, middle and outside linebackers. On a blitz the linebackers take special pleasure in going after the quarterback.

SACK THE QUARTERBACK SALSA AND BEEF FAJITAS

2 pounds flank steak
4 tablespoons fresh lime juice
4 tablespoons tequila
1 teaspoon chili powder
1 teaspoon dried oregano
1/2 teaspoon ground cumin
1/4 teaspoon black pepper
16 green onions, including green tops
16 flour tortillas, approximately 10" in diameter
4 cups romaine lettuce, shredded

SALSA

6-8 tomatoes, soft and ripe
Juice of 1 orange
2-3 green onions, chopped
1 medium white onion, finely chopped
Fresh green Anaheim chiles, finely chopped
Fresh yellow wax chiles, finely chopped
1 clove garlic, minced
Fresh cilantro

A sack is the attempt to tackle or otherwise dump the quarterback for a loss while he is attempting to pass. The middle linebacker, located behind and between the defensive tackles is the defensive quarterback in the 4-3 alignment.

PRE-GAME:
Slice steak against the grain into 1/2" wide strips.
In a large, shallow glass dish, combine lime juice, tequila, chili powder, oregano, cumin and black pepper.
Add the steak strips and green onions and toss well.
Marinate at least 30 minutes or longer.
SALSA: Remove skins by placing tomatoes in boiling water for 30 seconds. Immerse in pot of cold water and squeeze juice from tomatoes; finely chop. Add orange juice, onions, chiles, garlic and cilantro to tomato pulp and juice. Chill salsa. Serve, however, at room temperature.

SECOND QUARTER:
Warm flour tortillas by placing in a 400-degree oven for 3 minutes. They may also be steamed in a cloth towel and placed in vegetable steamer basket for 6-10 minutes over 1"-2" boiling water. Cover pot.
Five minutes before the *Half*, place meat strips in the center of the broiler, laying the green onions to one side. Broil one minute, each side. The steak should be medium rare and the onions lightly charred. Cut the steak strips into pieces approximately an inch long.

HALF-TIME:
Set out bowls of steak pieces, shredded lettuce, green onions and salsa. Have fans build their fajitas on the flour tortillas.

Yield: 8 servings

RUSHING THE PASSER ROAST BEEF PASTA

- 1 (3-pound) beef chuck roast
- 3 teaspoons salt
- 1/4 cup flour
- 1/4 cup olive oil
- 2 cups hot water
- 1/4 teaspoon garlic powder
- 1 teaspoon onion powder
- 2 bay leaves
- 1 teaspoon celery salt
- 1-1/2 teaspoons black pepper
- 2 teaspoons sugar
- 1/2 teaspoon red pepper, crushed
- 1 teaspoon beau monde
- 1/2 teaspoon oregano
- 2 teaspoons rosemary
- 1/8 teaspoon nutmeg
- 1/2 teaspoon basil
- 4 (6-ounce) cans tomato paste
- 1 quart water
- 1 cup red wine
- 1/2 cup stuffed olives, sliced
- 2 cups fresh mushrooms, sliced
- 4 anchovy fillets

PRE-GAME:

Season roast with salt; dredge with flour.
Using a Dutch oven or large pot, brown roast on all sides in hot oil. Add hot water; cover and cook slowly for 3 hours in 325-degree oven or until meat almost falls apart.
Tear into small pieces with a fork.
Add remaining ingredients and cook at least 1 hour.

FIRST QUARTER:

Simmer sauce in Dutch oven.

SECOND QUARTER:

Bring water to rolling boil in large kettle, add 1 teaspoon olive oil and 1/2 teaspoon salt. Add pasta to the water, maintaining a rolling boil. (Do not add pasta all at once or it can become sticky.) When cooked to desired texture, al dente, drain in colander. Rinse with cold and then hot water.
Place at least half the sauce in another saucepan. Add drained pasta to the Dutch oven filled with half the meat sauce. Pour any additional sauce from the saucepan until your meat sauce and pasta have the right consistency.

Yield: 3-1/2 quarts

Note: Freeze remaining sauce. Here's a tip to save time: Open two or more plastic bags. When measuring the spices measure same amount into each of the plastic bags and label. The next time you make this dish use one of the pre-measured bags.

> *The outside linebacker is generally a little lighter and faster than the other linebackers. His job is to go after the quarterback or stop the run on passing plays.*

CORNERBACK CHILI

1 pound pinto beans, cooked until soft
2 onions, chopped
2 garlic cloves, chopped
6 shallots
1 (7-ounce) can chopped green chiles
3 pounds ground chuck (chili grind)
1 pound ground sausage
1 (l-pound) can baked beans
1 (4-ounce) jar of chopped pimiento
3 (l pound 14-ounce) cans tomatoes
1/2 pound fresh mushrooms, sliced
1 red bell pepper, chopped
1 (9-ounce) can sliced or whole black olives
1/2 cup parsley, minced
1 (12-ounce) bottle chili sauce
2-3 tablespoons salt
1 tablespoon garlic salt
2 teaspoons pepper
1 tablespoon oregano
2 tablespoons chili powder

PRE-GAME:

Brown ground chuck; add onions, shallots, and garlic.
Brown sausage, drain.
Place all ingredients in a large Dutch oven or pot.
Simmer on low heat for two hours, stirring occasionally.
Be careful it doesn't burn. May also be heated in 350-degree oven.

FIRST QUARTER:

Reheat on very low heat.

There are two cornerbacks positioned behind the linebackers. They guard the wide receivers either man-to-man or by guarding zones. These members of the defensive secondary are sometimes called defensive halfbacks.

DEFENSVIE BACK BEEF BOURGUIGNON

5 pounds beef chuck, cut in 1-1/2" pieces
3/4 cup flour
2 teaspoons salt
1/2 teaspoon pepper
1 teaspoon savory
1/4 cup margarine
1/2 cup olive oil
1/2 cup brandy
1/2 pound bacon, diced
3 cloves garlic, crushed
3 cups carrots, coarsely chopped
4 cups leeks, coarsely chopped
6 cups yellow onions, chopped
1 cup parsley, chopped
2 bay leaves
3/4 teaspoons thyme
2 tablespoons tomato paste
3-1/2 cups red zinfandel wine
3 cans beef bouillion
2 (1-pound) cans whole onions, drained
1-1/2 pounds mushrooms, thickly sliced
1/4 cup margarine
Juice of 1 lemon
Salt and pepper to taste

Combine flour, salt, pepper and savory in paper bag. Coat beef with mixture. Shake off excess.

In a large, heavy skillet, brown meat on all sides in margarine and oil. This will have to be done in several batches adding margarine and oil as needed. Place browned meat in 5-quart casserole or large roasting pan. De-glaze skillet by pouring warmed brandy into it, lighting the brandy with a match, and stirring to loosen particles. Pour over meat.

In same skillet, add bacon, garlic, carrots, leeks, chopped onions and parsley. Stir until bacon and vegetables are lightly browned. Add bay leaves, thyme and tomato paste to skillet, stir and add to beef. Add wine and enough bouillion to barely cover meat mixture.
Cover casserole and bake 2 hours at 350 degrees, stirring occasionally. Add more bouillion if necessary.

Saute mushrooms in 1/4 cup margarine until lightly browned. Sprinkle with lemon juice. Add mushrooms and onions to beef and cook 1 more hour, or until beef is tender. Refrigerate. Skim any fat from surface of casserole and remove bay leaves. This dish also freezes well.

FIRST QUARTER KICKOFF:
Begin heating casserole early so it will be warm by *Half-Time*.
Warm in oven at 300 degrees. Be sure to remove hardened fat before reheating

Serving suggestions: Brown rice or baked Hungarian noodles.

Yield: 12 servings

The two cornerbacks are members of the defensive backfield. They are charged with stopping the pass or the run. These players are positioned 5-10 yards behind the line of scrimmage.

SAFETY
SAVORY VEGETABLE SOUP

2 pounds pot roast, trim fat
Garlic powder
Olive oil
1/3-1/2 package barley
4 large carrots, grated
1 large onion, chopped
3 stalks celery plus leaves, cleaned and chopped
4-6 large cloves garlic
1 red chili pepper
2 strips parsley
3 large (1-pound 28-ounce) can tomatoes, chopped
1 box cherry tomatoes, cleaned, stems removed (optional)
2 cups red wine
4-6 cups water
Salt and pepper to taste

PRE-GAME:
Place meat in skillet, sprinkle with garlic powder and brown in olive oil. Transfer meat to Dutch oven. Add remaining ingredients. Bring to boil. Place in oven 3 hours at 350 degrees.

FIRST QUARTER:
Simmer soup on low heat or heat in oven.

Two safeties line up 7 to 10 yards from the line of scrimmage. Since safeties are located farthest from the line of scrimmage they are charged with stopping the long play—breaking up the long pass or a running play. Think of them like the centerfielders in baseball. The strong safety is on the same side of the field as the offensive tight end.

FREE-SAFETY SEASONED MEATLOAF

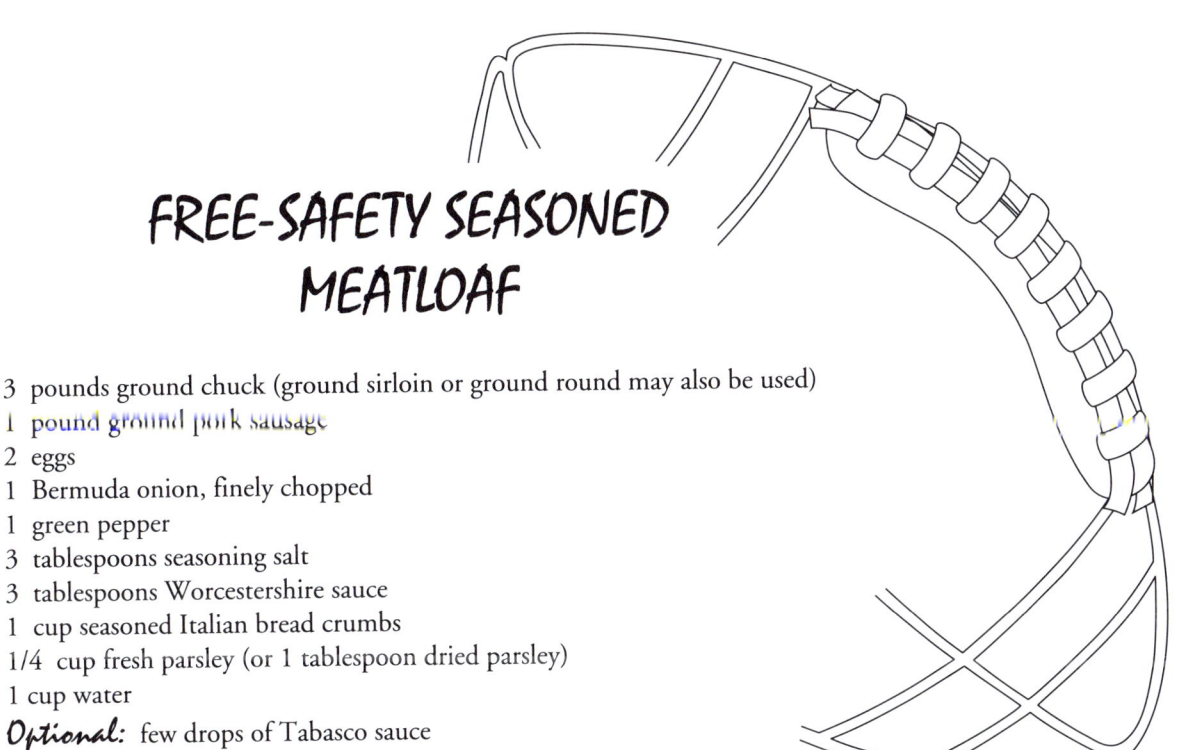

3 pounds ground chuck (ground sirloin or ground round may also be used)
1 pound ground pork sausage
2 eggs
1 Bermuda onion, finely chopped
1 green pepper
3 tablespoons seasoning salt
3 tablespoons Worcestershire sauce
1 cup seasoned Italian bread crumbs
1/4 cup fresh parsley (or 1 tablespoon dried parsley)
1 cup water

Optional: few drops of Tabasco sauce
3 hard-cooked eggs, chopped

PRE-GAME:

Mix all ingredients.
The secret of a good meatloaf is to mix the water in very well.
Place in a loaf pan.
Bake at 400 degrees for 1 hour 15 minutes, basting frequently.

Yield: 5-6 servings

Note: For a variation you may wish to layer half the ingredients in the pan. Top with 1 can of leaf spinach, drained or fresh spinach leaves and 1/2 cup of sliced green olives stuffed with pimiento.
Layer remaining meat mixture.

The weak-side safety is free to assist other team members with their coverage.

THE BREAD AND BUTTER OF THE GAME

Basic to football are the rules--keeping or breaking them. After this section you'll be able to make the call on key plays and penalties. There's still plenty to learn before you're in a league with the officials, but you'll have enough knowledge to enjoy the game.

Basic to most meals is the "staff of life" or bread. The yeast and quick breads are as easy-to-prepare as the herb and ingredient-stuffed French breads. If working with yeast is as unfamiliar as the NFL rule book than you'll enjoy tackling Touchdown Rolls for a game-winning effort.

THROW A BLOCK BACON CHEESE BREAD

2 (20-inch) loaves French bread
1/2 cup yellow onion, chopped
1/4 pound margarine
3-4 tablespoons prepared mustard
2 tablespoons poppy seeds
1 pound Swiss cheese, sliced
16 slices bacon

PRE-GAME:
Remove most of the crust from top of bread.
Slice at 1-inch intervals almost through bread.
Saute onion in margarine; add mustard and poppy seeds.
Spoon mixture into loaf cuts.
Insert cheese slices. Arrange bacon over top of loaf.

SECOND QUARTER:
Bake on cookie sheet uncovered at 350 degrees for 10-15 minutes or until cheese melts and bacon is crisp.

Note: Bread may be wrapped in foil and frozen. If placed in oven frozen it may take 30 or more minutes to bake.

A block occurs when an offensive or defensive player uses any part of his body, above the knees, to hinder an opponent. Arms must be kept close to the body. Using the face mask or front part of the helmet to begin a block is called "butt blocking." Illegal use of the hands results in a 5-yard penalty plus automatic first down. Illegal use of the hands on offense (holding) results in a 10-yard penalty.

OFF-SETTING PENALTIES ONION HERB BREAD

- 1 package dry yeast
- 1/4 cup warm water
- 1 cup cottage cheese
- 2 tablespoons sugar
- 3 tablespoons onions
- 2 teaspoons dill seed
- 1 tablespoon margarine
- 1/3 teaspoon baking soda
- 1 teaspoon salt
- 1 egg
- 2-1/4 to 2-1/2 cups flour, sifted
- 1/2 cup margarine
- 1-1/2 teaspoons celery seed

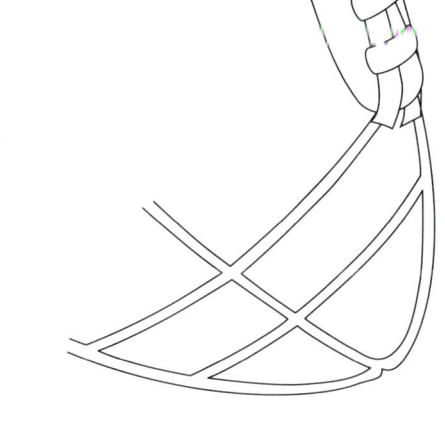

PRE-GAME:

Dissolve yeast in warm water.
Combine cottage cheese, sugar, onion, dill seed, margarine, soda, salt and egg in a large bowl. Add yeast.
Gradually add flour, enough to make a stiff dough.
Mix well. Cover and allow to rise until double. Punch down.
Place dough in greased 9" x 5" loaf pan.
Let dough rise until doubled.
Bake at 350 degrees 40-50 minutes.
When removed from pan, top with melted butter mixed with celery seeds.

Yield: 1 loaf

OFF-SETTING PENALTIES
When both teams are guilty of rule infractions on the same down the penalties will cancel each other out.

UNSPORTSMANLIKE ONION, CHEESE AND CHILE BREAD

10 to 12 small French rolls
1 pound Jack cheese, shredded
1 (8-ounce) can tomato sauce
1 (4-ounce) can diced green chiles

6 green onions, finely chopped
2 tablespoons olive oil
2 cloves garlic, minced
2 ounces Parmesan cheese, grated

PRE-GAME:

Split rolls in half, lengthwise. Scoop out soft bread leaving about 1/2-inch crust shell.
Combine Jack cheese, tomato sauce, chiles, green onions, oil and garlic in large bowl.
Spoon equal amounts of cheese mixture into bread shells.
Sprinkle each with Parmesan cheese.
Arrange on baking sheet and bake at 425 degrees 10 minutes.

SECOND QUARTER:

If the oven is available you may wish to bake these 10 minutes before the *Half* instead of earlier.
Sprinkle with minced green onions and serve hot.

Yield: 8-10 servings

UNSPORTSMANLIKE CONDUCT
Behavior that is contrary to the "generally understood principles of sportsmanship" may result in a 15-yard penalty.

HANDOFF
HEARTY HERB BREAD

6 cups all-purpose flour
2 packages active dry yeast
4 tablespoons sugar
1 tablespoon salt
3/4 cup dry milk
4 teaspoons celery or caraway seeds

2 teaspoons sage
1/2 teaspoon nutmeg
1-1/2 cups milk
4 tablespoons shortening
1/2 cup water
2 eggs

PRE-GAME:
Set 2 cups of flour aside.
In large bowl combine remaining flour, yeast, sugar, salt, dry milk, celery or caraway seeds, sage and nutmeg. Scald milk. Heat shortening, water and milk (to 120-130 degrees).
Add to mixture in large bowl. Add 2 beaten eggs and reserved flour as needed. Form and place in loaf pan.
Glaze with beaten egg white; bake at 400 degrees for 35 minutes.

HALF-TIME:
Slice and serve.

> **HANDOFF**
> The exchange of the ball from one offensive player to another is known as a 'handoff'.

FREE KICK
HERB-BUTTERED FRENCH BREAD

2 loaves French Bread, sliced
1/2 cup butter
1 tablespoon chives, finely chopped

1 tablespoon parsley, finely chopped
1/2 teaspoon tarragon, crushed
1/2 teaspoon chervil, crushed

PRE-GAME:
Melt butter and mix herbs together.
Slice French bread and spread herb-butter mixture on each slice, front and back.

SECOND QUARTER:
Place bread slices on baking sheet in 350 degree oven 15-20 minutes.

> **FREE KICK**
> If a free kick is granted the offensive team, the defensive players may not interfere with the kicker. This may occur as a kick-off, kick after a fair catch or a kick after a safety. The kicker may employ a place kick, drop kick, or punt. A punt, however, cannot be used on a kick-off.

FORWARD PASS FOCCACIA BREAD

BREAD

2 (1-pound) loaves frozen bread dough
2 cloves garlic, slivered
1 teaspoon kosher salt

1 tablespoon fresh rosemary
or 1 teaspoon dried rosemary

ROSEMARY-OLIVE OIL

5-6 tablespoons extra virgin olive oil
1 clove garlic, sliced or crushed

1 sprig fresh rosemary or
1 teaspoon dried

PRE-GAME:
ROSEMARY/OLIVE OIL: (Make one day ahead of time.) Place garlic and rosemary in olive oil.

BREAD: Allow frozen dough to thaw at room temperature for about an hour or follow package directions. Roll into rectangular shape on floured bread board or between two pieces of floured wax paper. Oil cookie sheet lightly with the rosemary-olive oil and place dough on top.
With knife, score bread in diagonal cuts without going through bread. Lines should be approximately 1-1/2" a part.
Brush top generously with seasoned olive oil. Stud bread with garlic slivers; sprinkle with rosemary and kosher salt.
Bake at 375 degrees for 20-25 minutes or until golden brown.
Remove from oven and cool on rack.

SECOND QUARTER:
May be served warm or at room temperature.
Cut along diagonal strips. Serve in 5"-7" lengths.

Note: May be made a day ahead of time.

Can you imagine, when the forward pass was allowed, some feared it would ruin the game? That's a great example supporting the importance of change.

FORWARD PASS
A team in possession of the ball may throw the ball on each play. The pass must be thrown behind the line of scrimmage or it's declared an illegal forward pass. Eligible receivers include wide receivers, the tight end or the running backs.

The quarterback is eligible to receive a pass in certain instances. Of course, any defensive team member is eligible to receive a forward pass, but then it's called an interception.

LATERAL PASS MOZZARELLA LOAF

2 loaves French bread
1 (8-ounce) package cream cheese, softened
2 cups mozzarella cheese, shredded
4 tablespoons margarine, softened
1/2 cup chopped green onions, using 2" of their tops
1 teaspoon garlic salt

PRE-GAME:
Slice bread in half lengthwise.
Soften cream cheese and mozzarella.
Add remaining ingredients to cheese mixture.
Spread evenly along the four halves.
Wrap in foil.

SECOND QUARTER:
Preheat oven to 400 degrees. Bake for 10-15 minutes.

LATERAL OR BACKWARD PASS
A team may pass the ball to either side or backward when it is in possession of the ball. If dropped, either team may recover the ball. If the opposing team gains possession it becomes a dead ball and this changes possession of the ball.

ONSIDE KICK BREAD STICKS

1-3/4 cups all purpose flour
3/4 cup Parmesan cheese
1 tablespoon sugar
1 teaspoon salt
1 package active dry yeast

2/3 cup water
1/4 cup salad oil
1 egg
1 teaspoon sesame seed

PRE-GAME:
Combine 1 cup flour with the cheese, sugar, salt and yeast in a mixing bowl.
In small pan, heat 2/3 cup water with oil until lukewarm.
Using an electric mixer at medium speed, gradually add liquid to flour mixture and beat 2 minutes, scraping the bowl.
Add 3/4 cup flour to make a soft dough.
Beat 2 more minutes at medium speed.
Knead on floured surface 5 minutes. Dough will not be smooth because of the cheese. Place dough in greased bowl; cover with warm, damp towel.
Let it rise in warm place (80-85 degrees) for 1 hour or until doubled.
Punch down.
Roll out, cut with serrated knife; place strips on greased cookie sheet.
Beat 1 egg and brush on sticks; sprinkle with sesame seeds.
Bake for 20 minutes in a 350-degree oven; remove and allow to cool.

ONSIDE KICK
A short kick-off by which the kicking team hopes to regain possession of the ball. The ball must go at least 10 yards before the kicking team can recover. If it travels less than 10 yards the receiving team retains the ball.

This tactic may be tried late in a game when the kicking team needs to retain possession of the ball to score. If the onside kick is unsuccessful, it ususally provides excellent field advantage to the receiving team.

CLIPPING CORN BREAD SQUARES

1 sweet, medium, white, Spanish onion
1/4 cup margarine
1 (8-1/2 ounce) box corn muffin mix
1 egg, beaten
1/3 cup milk
1 cup cream style corn
2-3 drops Tabasco sauce
1 cup sour cream
1/4 teaspoon salt
1/4 teaspoon dill weed
1 cup sharp cheddar cheese, grated

PRE-GAME:

Chop onion and saute slowly in margarine. Set aside.
Combine muffin mix, egg, milk, corn and Tabasco.
Pour into buttered 8" square pan.
Add sour cream, salt, dill weed and half the cheese to sauteed onions.
(You may wish to add more sour cream and dill weed to taste.)
Spread over batter.
Sprinkle with remaining cheese.

SECOND QUARTER:

Bake for 30-35 minutes at 425 degrees.

CLIPPING

How many times has your favorite team executed a brilliant running play, gaining needed yardage and more, only to be called for "clipping"? Plenty, I bet. Clipping occurs when a member of the opposing team throws his body across the back of an opponent's leg. A hit from the rear while an opponent is moving up from behind is also a "clip." Clipping results in a 15-yard penalty.

PERSONAL FOUL GOURMET FRENCH BREAD

1 loaf French bread, sliced lengthwise
Margarine
1 cup mayonnaise
1/2 cup green onions, finely chopped
1/2 cup Monterey Jack cheese, grated
1/2 teaspoon Worcestershire sauce
Paprika
Parmesan cheese

PRE-GAME:
Spread margarine on both lengths of bread.
Mix mayonnaise, onions, cheese and Worcestershire sauce.
Spread mixture on bread.
Sprinkle with paprika and Parmesan cheese.

SECOND QUARTER:
Bake on a cookie sheet at 350 degrees for approximately 15 minutes.

PERSONAL FOUL
The penalties for personal fouls or illegal hits are as follows:
15 yards
(automatic first down)
- Clipping
- Piling on
- Unnecessary roughness
- Butting, spearing or ramming an opponent

5 yards
(automatic first down)
- Running into the kicker

HONEY BUTTER

1 stick butter or margarine
1/2 cup powdered sugar
1/2 cup honey
1/2-1 teaspoon cinnamon

PRE-GAME:
Beat all ingredients with electric mixer until light and fluffy.
Store in refrigerator.

HALF-TIME:
Serve with raisin, walnut and various fruit breads or with white and whole wheat bread.

AUTOMATIC FIRST DOWN
AUTOMATIC HONEY-SESAME BREAD

Automatic bread machines are becoming increasing popular. Here's a recipe using machines for both 1 pound and 1-1/2 pound loaves.

INGREDIENTS	1 POUND LOAF	1-1/2 POUND LOAF
Water	3/4 cup	1-1/4 cups
White Bread Flour	1-1/2 cups	2-1/4 cups
Wheat Bread Flour	1/2 cup	3/4 cup
Dry Milk	1 tablespoon	2 tablespoons
Salt	1/4 teaspoon	1/3 teaspoon
Butter	1 tablespoon	1-1/2 tablespoons
Honey	2 tablespoons	3 tablespoons
Sesame Seeds	1/4 cup	1/2 cup
Yeast		
Rapid:	1-1/4 teaspoons	2 teaspoons
Active Dry:	2 teaspoons	3 teaspoons

PRE-GAME:
Follow manufacturer's directions for the bread machine. Adhere to sequence of ingredients, especially when water or yeast are to be added.

Note: Use honey butter spread on page 116. This spread is excellent on other types of whole grain breads.

The following fouls result in lost yardage plus an automatic first down:

5 yards
Defensive holding
Illegal use of the hands
Running into the kicker

15 yards
Piling on
Roughing the kicker
Roughing the passer

FAIR CATCH
COTTAGE CHEESE BEER BREAD

2-3/4 cups flour
1/2 teaspoon salt
2 tablespoons sugar
1 package rapid-rise yeast
1 teaspoon cracked pepper
1/2 cup + 2 tablespoons grated Parmesan cheese
1 cup low-fat cottage cheese, warmed slightly
1 cup beer, warmed (or low fat milk)

PRE-GAME:
Combine flour, salt, sugar, yeast, pepper and Parmesan cheese.
Blend in food processor with metal blade.
Add cottage cheese and beer; mix briefly.
Grease a 6-cup casserole, souffle dish or a 5"x 9" loaf pan.
Pour in mixture; cover; allow to rise in a warm place for 45 minutes.
Bake at 350 degrees 40-50 minutes until brown and crusty.

FAIR CATCH
After a kick the opposing player may raise one hand at arm's length above his head. This signals a "fair catch." He can now catch the ball without being tackled. The ball is dead on that spot and he may not run or advance the ball.

Fair catch interference results in a 15-yard penalty. Invalid fair catch signal penalizes a team 5 yards.

OFFSIDE ONION CAKE

- 1 package hot roll mix
- 4 large yellow onions, peeled (approximately 8 cups)
- 1/2 cup margarine
- 2 cups sour cream
- 3 eggs
- 1/2 teaspoon salt
- 1/2 teaspoon caraway seeds

PRE-GAME:
Prepare roll dough according to directions.
While dough rises, slice onions. In large skillet, saute onions in margarine slowly until limp and golden. Cool slightly.
In mixer beat sour cream, eggs and salt thoroughly.
Add onion mixture.
When dough has doubled, punch down and allow to rest 10 minutes.
Roll out dough on lightly floured board in rectangle 2" larger than pan.
Line greased 9" x 13" pan with dough, turning up an inch on all sides.
Pour onion filling over dough.
Sprinkle with caraway seeds. Refrigerate.

FIRST-QUARTER:
Bake 55 minutes in a 350-degree oven or until crust is browned and custard set.

HALF-TIME:
Cut into squares, serve warm.

Yield: 12 servings

OFFSIDE
A 5-yard penalty for offsides can occur when any part of a players' body is beyond his own line of scrimmage or free-kick line when the ball is snapped.

PASS INTERFERENCE PEPPER, PARMESAN, PAPRIKA TWISTS

1 (10-ounce) package soft bread twists
1 egg, beaten
3 tablespoons Parmesan cheese
1/4 teaspoon black pepper
1/4 teaspoon cayenne pepper
1/2 teaspoon paprika

PRE-GAME:
Roll out dough according to package directions.
Mix Parmesan, peppers and paprika. Dip twists in egg followed by cheese mixture. Bake on ungreased baking sheet at 375 degrees, 10-15 minutes.

SECOND QUARTER:
If baked earlier, bread may be warmed in oven 5-10 minutes on low temperature. Wrap twists in foil.

Yield: 8 bread twists

PASS INTERFERENCE

Illegal interference with a player's chance to catch a forward pass or make an interception results in various penalties. Offensive pass interference is a 10-yard penalty from the previous spot. Defensive pass interference is an automatic first down where the foul occurred. If interference occurs in the end zone, the ball is placed on the defense's 1-yard line. If the previous spot was inside the defense's one-yard line, the penalty is half the distance to the goal.

TOUCHDOWN ROLLS

1 cup solid
   vegetable shortening
1 cup sugar
1 teaspoon salt
2 eggs, beaten
2 packages active dry yeast
6 cups all-purpose flour

PRE-GAME:

In large bowl place shortening, sugar and salt. Pour 2 cups boiling water over mixture. Let shortening melt. Add beaten eggs and stir together well. In 1 cup warm water dissolve 2 packages of yeast. Mix yeast with egg/sugar mixture. Stir in flour and mix well.
Refrigerate overnight. Remove from refrigerator.
Grease muffin tins. (Flour hands to avoid sticking.)
Pinch off three balls of dough, roll slightly and place in each hole.
Allow rolls to rise until doubled, approximately 3-4 hours.
Bake at 425 degrees for 7 minutes.

Yield: 4 to 4-1/2 dozen

Note: If rolls have doubled in size and you wish to wait and bake them during the end of the **Second Quarter**, place in refrigerator covered to stop their rising. You may wish to bake ahead and then simply warm in foil a few minutes before the **Half**.

> **TOUCHDOWN**
> *A team scores 6 points when it puts the football across the opponents' goal line by running or pasing the ball.*

SUDDEN DEATH DESSERTS

"Sudden death" occurs when the score is tied at the end of regulation play for all NFL games. The team scoring first during successive 15-minute overtime periods becomes the winner.

In 1958 Dad and I watched what some considered, "the greatest game ever played". A sudden-death playoff decided the outcome. Johnny Unitas quarterbacked the Baltimore Colts to victory over the New York Giants and became the game's MVP (Most Valuable Player). He remains one of my heroes today, ranking almost up there with Dad.

Prior to 1958 the names of Jim Thorpe, Don Hutson, Bob Waterfield, Sammy Baugh and others were written into the record books. However, the Colts' December victory was a benchmark in football for me. That's the reason only players after that date have been mentioned.

After the final play the teams head toward their respective locker rooms. Let's learn more about the players who have enriched the game. They've whetted our appetites for more spectacular passes and 90-plus yard runs.

Coincidentally, it's dessert time! Try some of these rich confections and traditional favorites showcasing a partial list of my football heroes past and present.

PECAN CHOCOLATE CHIP COOKIES

1 cup buttery solid vegetable shortening
2 sticks margarine
2 cups sugar
1 cup brown sugar
4 eggs
4-1/2 cups flour
2 teaspoons soda
1 teaspoon hot water
1 teaspoon vanilla
2 (12-ounce) packages semi-sweet chocolate chips
2 cups pecans, chopped

PRE-GAME
Cream shortening, margarine, sugars and eggs.
Add flour, soda, hot water and vanilla to creamed mixture.
Mix well.
Add chocolate chips and pecans.
Drop by teaspoons on greased cookie sheets.
Bake at 375 degrees 10-12 minutes.

Yield: 8 dozen cookies

Note: Cookie dough may be rolled in foil and frozen. Cut to bake.

STEVE LARGENT
Next to "mom and apple pie" what's more wholesome or sought after than chocolate chip cookies? Perhaps Steve Largent of the Seattle Seahawks. As a wide receiver, known for great hands, he caught a record-setting number of consecutive touchdowns. On and off the field, Steve Largent is a stand-out. Steve exemplifies the best in men and pro football.

CHOCOLATE PEPPER COOKIES

3 cups flour
1-1/4 cups cocoa
1/2 teaspoon salt
1-1/2 teaspoons cinnamon
1/4 teaspoon black pepper
1/4 teaspoon cayenne pepper

1-1/2 cups butter, softened
2 cups sugar
2 eggs
1 tablespoon vanilla
Powdered sugar

PRE-GAME
Sift together flour, cocoa, salt, cinnamon, black and cayenne pepper.
Cream butter, sugar, eggs and vanilla.
Mix creamed mixture with sifted ingredients.
Form into logs and roll in waxed paper; refrigerate 2 hours.
Slice in 1/4" thickness. Bake on cookie sheets at 350 degrees for 6-7 minutes. Cool.
Make football stencils—helmet, football, numbers, etc.
Use your football imagination.
Place stencils on top cookie. Dust with powdered sugar.
Remove stencil.

KICKERS
The point-after touchdown and the three-point field goal has determined many a game. Some of the great kickers have been: George Blanda, Gino Cappelletti, Lou Groza, Mark Moseley, Jan Stenerud and Jim Turner.

DOUBLE CHOCOLATE CRUMBLE CRISP BARS

1/2 cup margarine
1/4 cup sugar
2 eggs
1 teaspoon vanilla
3/4 cup all-purpose flour
1/2 cup pecans, chopped
2 tablespoons unsweetened cocoa powder
1/4 teaspoon baking powder
1/4 teaspoon salt
2 cups small marshmallows

TOPPING

1 (6-ounce) package semi-sweet chocolate chips
1 cup peanut butter
1-1/2 cups crisp rice cereal

PRE-GAME:
Cream margarine and sugar, beat in eggs and vanilla.
Stir flour, nuts, cocoa, baking powder and salt into egg mixture.
Spread in bottom of greased 13" x 9" x 2" baking pan.
Bake at 350 degrees for 15-20 minutes.
Sprinkle marshmallows evenly on top; bake 3 minutes more. Cool.

TOPPING: In small saucepan combine chocolate chips and peanut butter; cook and stir over heat until chocolate is melted. Stir in cereal. Spread mixture over cooked bars. Chill.
Cut into bars and refrigerate.

Yield: 3-4 dozen

GEORGE HALAS
George Halas ("Papa Bear") doubled as both a football player (with the Decatur Staleys) and then as coach for the Chicago Bears. In fact his coaching career remains the longest in pro football. Halas perfected the "T" formation attack still used today. Employing this offense for the first time, the Bears smothered their opponents 73-0. As player, coach or team owner, George Halas served pro football for over six decades.

CHOCOLATE CHIP BARS

2-3/4 cups sifted flour
2-1/2 teaspoons baking powder
1/2 teaspoon salt
2/3 cup oil
1 pound brown sugar
3 eggs
1 cup walnuts, chopped
1 (8-ounce) package semi-sweet chocolate chips
1 teaspoon vanilla

PRE-GAME:
Mix flour, baking powder and salt.
In another mixing bowl, combine oil and brown sugar. Mix.
Add eggs one at a time, beating well after each addition.
Add dry ingredients, nuts, chocolate chips and vanilla.
Pour into shallow, greased pan and bake at 350 degrees for 35 minutes.
When cool, cut into small bars.

Note: This is an easy alternative to chocolate cookies and one that will be enjoyed just as much.

JOE NAMATH
Joe Namath led an underdog New York Jets team to victory in Super Bowl III. The Jets' win brought a needed boost to the fledgling American Football League against the National Football League's team. Joe's personality and ability made him popular both on and off the field. Shortly after his arrival in New York he acquired the nickname, "Broadway Joe." He even owned a bar with that moniker.

QUICK COOKIES

1 (6-ounce) package chocolate chips
1 (6-ounce) package butterscotch chips
1 cup peanuts
1 cup chow mein noodles

PRE-GAME:
Melt chips in double boiler.
Stir in peanuts and noodles.
Drop by teaspoonfuls on waxed paper to cool.

Note: Subsitute peanut butter chips for butterscotch, if desired.

> **JAWORSKI TO QUICK**
> *In a memorable 1985 sudden-death situation between the Philadelphia Eagles and the Atlanta Falcons, quarterback Ron Jaworski handed the ball to Mike Quick who ran for 99 yards and a place in the NFL record books.*

> **O. J. SIMPSON**
> *O J "the Juice," Simpson was a talented running back for the Buffalo Bills. His 23 touchdowns in one season tie him for second place in the record books. During Simpson's tenure the team was nicknamed the Buffalo Bills' Electric Company— their team turned on the "electrical juice."*

ORANGE JEWEL COOKIES

1-1/2 cups flour
1/2 teaspoon baking powder
1/2 teaspoon soda
1/2 teaspoon salt
2/3 cup buttery solid vegetable shortening
2/3 cup sugar
2/3 cup brown sugar
2 eggs
1 teaspoon vanilla
1-1/2 cups quick oats
1 cup coconut, flaked or shredded
3 tablespoons orange juice (optional)
1-1/2 cups jellied orange candy slices (10 ounces), sliced

PRE-GAME:
Sift flour, baking powder, soda and salt.
Cream lard and sugar. Beat eggs and vanilla into creamed mixture.
Stir in sifted ingredients. Add oats, coconut, orange juice and orange slices; mix.
Shape into balls. Flatten on cookie sheet.
Bake at 375 degrees for 10-12 minutes or longer.

Yield: 3 dozen

PEANUT BUTTER COOKIES

1/2 cup butter
1/2 cup brown sugar
1/2 cup sugar
1/2 cup peanut butter
1 egg
1/2 teaspoon vanilla
1/2 teaspoon salt
1-1/2 cups flour
1 teaspoon soda

PRE-GAME:
Mix first 7 ingredients.
Add sifted flour and soda.
Roll dough into spoon-size balls. Dip fork in flour and press down ball, crisscrossing to form a design.
Bake on greased cookie sheet at 350 degrees for 10 minutes.

CHARTER CARAMEL COOKIES

1 package German chocolate cake mix
3/4 cup butter
1 cup evaporated milk
1 cup walnuts
1 (12-ounce) package semi-sweet chocolate chips
Approximately 50 caramels

PRE-GAME:
Mix dry cake mix with butter, 1/3 cup evaporated milk and 3/4 cup walnuts. Pour half of mixture into 9" x 12" cake pan.
Bake 10 minutes at 350 degrees.
Sprinkle chocolate chips over baked cake mix.
Melt 50 caramels with 1/3 cup evaporated milk (or more if needed).
Pour caramel mixture over top of chocolate chips.
Place remaining cake mixture on top of caramel mixture and bake for 20 minutes at 350 degrees.
Sprinkle with 1/4 cup walnuts.
Slice when cool.

Several flight attendants at Alaska Airlines would make these caramel cookies for the Seattle Seahawk charters.

WALTER PAYTON
Walter Payton played halfback for the Chicago Bears. Although he retired in 1987, he's still the all-time rushing leader (with 16,726 yards).

GINGERSNAP BARS

3/4 cup margarine
1 cup sugar
1 egg
1/4 cup light molasses
2 teaspoons soda

1/2 teaspoon salt
1/2 teaspoon cinnamon
1/2 teaspoon ginger
1/2 teaspoon cloves
2-1/2 cups flour

GLAZE

3/4 cup powdered sugar
1 tablespoon margarine, melted

1 tablespoon milk
1/2 teaspoon vanilla

PRE-GAME

Combine margarine and sugar. Add egg and molasses to sugar mixture.
Blend soda, salt, cinnamon, ginger, cloves and flour.
Mix into heavy dough. Divide into 6 pieces.
Shape each into a 12" rope. Place on cookie sheet.
Flatten rope. Brush with water. Sprinkle with sugar.
Bake at 350 degrees 12-15 minutes.
Cut diagonally into 3/4" bar.
DO NOT separate until cool.
Drizzle with glaze while slightly warm.

GLAZE: Mix ingredients.

JOHNNY UNITAS
My love of football started in 1958 watching Johnny Unitas, number 19, quarterback the Baltimore (now Indianapolis) Colts to many victories. Unitas received the snap for 18 seasons. Three times he was named NFL Player of the Year. He played in ten Pro Bowl games, three NFL Championships and two Super Bowl games. His most enduring mark—throwing at least one touchdown pass in 47 straight games.

M-M-M-MONSTER COOKIES

1 pound brown sugar
2 cups white sugar
1/2 pound margarine
6 eggs
1/2 teaspoons vanilla
4 teaspoons baking soda
1-1/2 pound peanut butter

9 cups quick-cooking rolled oats
1 (8-ounce) package M&M's
1 (8-ounce) package M&M's with peanuts
1 (6-ounce) package chocolate chips
1 cup walnuts, chopped
1 cup shredded coconut
1 cup raisins (optional)

PRE-GAME:

Mix sugars and margarine.
Add eggs, vanilla, soda, peanut butter and rolled oats.
Stir in remaining ingredients.
Form into balls, flatten to 1/4" with a fork.
Bake at 350 degrees for 15-20 minutes.

(Yield: Depends on size you make these monsters.)

JOE GREEN
Mean Joe Green, defensive lineman for the Pittsburgh Steelers, didn't earn his nickname by being nice. He was tossed out of more than one game for being too aggressive. Spitting, punching, or being called for a late hit were all parts of his mean persona.

A LOT OF LEMON BARS

2 cups flour
2 sticks margarine
1/2 cup powdered sugar
4 eggs, slightly beaten
2 cups sugar

1 teaspoon baking powder
4 tablespoons flour
6 tablespoons lemon juice
1 lemon rind, grated

PRE-GAME:
Mix first three ingredients with fork or pastry blender.
Press into a 9"x 12" x 2" cake pan. Bake 20 minutes at 350 degrees.
Combine remaining ingredients and mix well.
Pour second mixture over hot crust.
Bake at 350 degrees for 25 minutes or until light brown around edges.
While slightly warm, sift powdered sugar over top.
When completely cooled, cut into squares or diamonds.
Lift from pan with narrow spatula.

RONNIE LOTT

Ronnie Lott is now a safety for the Los Angeles Raiders. He's best known for his years as a lineman with many winning San Francisco 49ers teams. Ronnie Lott has made lemons out of many of his opponent's plays with a record number of interceptions.

GERMAN CHOCOLATE AND CREAM CHEESE BROWNIES

1 (4 ounce) package German sweet chocolate
5 tablespoons margarine
1 (3-ounce) package cream cheese
1 cup sugar
3 eggs
1/2 cup plus 1 tablespoon unsifted flour
1-1/2 teaspoons vanilla
1-1/2 teaspoons baking powder
1/4 teaspoon salt
1/2 cup walnuts, coarsely chopped
1/4 teaspoon almond extract

PRE-GAME:

Melt chocolate and 3 tablespoons margarine over very low heat, stirring constantly. Cool.
Cream remaining margarine with cream cheese until soft.
Gradually add 1/4 cup sugar, creaming until light and fluffy.
Blend in 1 egg, 1 tablespoon flour and 1/2 teaspoon vanilla.
Set aside.
Beat remaining eggs until thick and light in color.
Gradually add remaining 3/4 cup sugar, beating until thickened; add baking powder, salt and remaining flour.
Blend in cooled chocolate mixture, nuts, almond extract and remaining 1 teaspoon vanilla. Measure 1 cup chocolate batter; set aside.
Spread remaining chocolate batter in greased 9" square pan. Top with cheese mixture. Drop chocolate batter that was set aside by tablespoons into cheese mixture; swirl with spatula to marble.
Bake at 350 degrees for 35-40 minutes. Cool and cut.

Yield: 20 brownies

JIM BROWN
Jim Brown's rushing record of 12,312 yards stood for almost twenty years. This alone attests to the greatness of this runner with the Cleveland Browns. From his first game as a rookie, Jim Brown never missed a game.

ROCKY ROAD BROWNIES

3/4 cup flour
1/4 teaspoon baking soda
1/4 teaspoon salt
1/3 cup margarine
3/4 cup sugar

2 tablespoons water
1 (12-ounce) package semi-sweet chocolate chips
2 teaspoons vanilla
2 eggs
1/2 cup chopped walnuts (optional)

ROCKY ROAD FROSTING

1/4 cup margarine
1/4 cup water
2 squares unsweetened chocolate
2 cups miniature marshmallows

2 cups powdered sugar
1 teaspoon vanilla
1/2 cup walnuts

DICK BUTKUS
Dick Butkus played linebacker for the Chicago Bears from 1965-73. Everyone who came up against him found a "rocky road." Biting, punching, or battering the opponent were some of his favorite tactics. He's known as one of the best linebackers who ever played the game.

PRE-GAME:
In small bowl combine flour, soda and salt.
In saucepan melt margarine. Add sugar and water. Bring to a boil and remove from heat. Add 1 cup chocolate chips and vanilla, stirring until melted and smooth.
Transfer chocolate mixture to large bowl.
Add eggs, one at a time, beating well after each addition.
Pour flour mixture into the chocolate mixture.
Stir in remaining chips and walnuts.
Spread mixture into greased 9" square baking pan.
Bake for 30-35 minutes in pre-heated 325-degree oven. Cool.

FROSTING: In sauce pan melt margarine in water. Add chocolate and 1 cup of marshmallows. Cool. Add powdered sugar and vanilla. Beat until smooth (approximately 2 minutes).
Stir in remaining marshmallows and nuts.
When brownies cool, frost with Rocky Road Frosting.

MEMORABLE CHOCOLATE MOUSSE CAKE

1 angel food cake	4 egg, separated
1 (12-ounce) package semi-sweet chocolate chips	2 tablespoons water
	1 cup whipping cream.

TOPPING
(Optional)

1 cup whipping cream	3/4 cup walnuts, chopped

PRE-GAME:
Melt chocolate chips over water in double boiler. Remove from heat; add one unbeaten egg yolk at a time. Cool.
Beat egg whites. When stiff, mix chocolate mixture with egg whites. In a separate bowl beat whipping cream and fold into chocolate mixture.
Cut or tear angel food cake into pieces and place half in bottom of 8" square pan. Pour half the chocolate mixture over cake pieces. Repeat. Refrigerate.

HALF-TIME:
Serve cake as is or top with additional whipped cream and chopped nuts.

MEMORABLE LINEMEN AND DEFENSIVE PLAYERS

These may not all be household names of football's past and present. Week after week linemen and defensive secondary players block, tackle, create the holes and/or snap the ball.

Dan Dierdorf
Bob Lilly
Howie Long
Ed (Too Tall) Jones
Lawrence Taylor
Jeff Van Note.

APPLE-PRALINE CAKE

4 cups apples, peeled and chopped (approximately 4 apples)
2 cups sugar
1/2 cup cooking oil
1 cup pecans

2 eggs, well beaten
2 cups flour
2 teaspoons soda
2 teaspoons cinnamon
1 teaspoon salt

PRALINE TOPPING

1 cup sugar
1/4 cup milk
1/4 teaspoon vanilla

2 teaspoons butter
1 cup pecans, chopped

PRE-GAME:
Mix all cake ingredients in order listed.
Bake in well-greased pan (bundt, tube, or rectangular) at 325 degrees for 1 hour.
Remove from oven. If using a bundt or tube pan, invert on rack.

PRALINE TOPPING:
Place 1/3 cup sugar and milk in large saucepan.
Cook slowly. In another pan cook 2/3 cup sugar on low heat; stir until melted.
Pour melted sugar slowly into milk and sugar that should be ready to boil. Mix while adding.
Cook slowly until firm-ball stage.
Remove from heat and add vanilla and butter.
Beat until mixture begins to thicken. Stir in pecans.
Pour or spoon out, quickly and carefully, some on top of the apple cake.
Spoon remaining batter, cookie-size, on waxed paper coated with butter. Pralines will set immediately.

ARCHIE MANNING
Pralines are as synonymous with Louisiana as the name Archie Manning is with the New Orleans Saints. He served as the "signal caller," or quarterback, during their early years as a franchise.

B AND B MULTI-MILLION DOLLAR CAKE

- 1 package yellow cake mix
- 1 small (3.4-ounce) package instant lemon pudding
- 4 eggs
- 1-1/2 cups nuts, chopped
- 3/4 cup oil
- 3/4 cup B & B (Benedictine and Brandy). Cream sherry or rum works too.
- Suggested fresh fruit: strawberries, kiwis, grapes, plums, and bananas (dip bananas in lemon juice).

AMBROSIA CREAM

- 1 cup whipping cream
- 1 teaspoon brandy
- 1 teaspoon Grand Mariner
- 1-1/2 teaspoon vanilla
- 2 tablespoons white sugar
- 2 tablespoons brown sugar
- 3 tablespoons sour cream

PRE-GAME:
Mix all ingredients except fruit and pour into greased bundt pan. Bake at 350 degrees for 40 minutes.

AMBROSIA CREAM: Whip cream, brandy, and Grand Mariner together for 30 seconds to 1 minute—until cream begins to thicken. Add sugar and sour cream and beat approximately 2 minutes or until soft peaks form.

HALF-TIME
Slice cake and serve with fruit and Ambrosia Cream.

Brandy and Benedictine are two liqueurs that can be used in this cake. When applying B and B to football you've got to think of the head-on collision between two rookies, Brian Bosworth and Bo Jackson. The Monday Night Football audience witnessed the $18.4 million meeting of these players in the end zone.

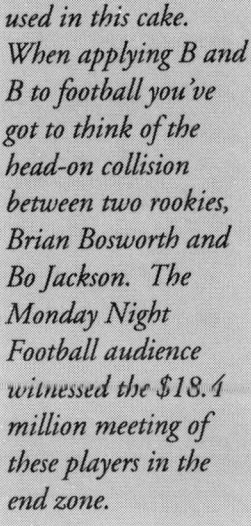

OLD-FASHIONED OATMEAL CAKE

1 stick margarine
1 cup raw quick-cook oats
1-1/4 cups boiling water
1 cup sugar
1 cup brown sugar
2 eggs

1-1/2 cups flour
1/2 teaspoon salt
1 teaspoon soda
1 teaspoon baking powder
1/2 teaspoon nutmeg
1 teaspoon cinnamon

FROSTING

6 tablespoons margarine
1/2 cup sugar
1 cup flaked coconut

1/2 cup evaporated milk
1/2 teaspoon vanilla
3/4 cup pecans, chopped

GEORGE BLANDA

George Blanda played professional football for 26 seasons. He began as a quarterback, but later became a kicker. At age 48, after playing for the Bears, Colts, Oilers and Raiders he retired.

This is one of my oldest recipes. I've been making it for 30 years—I won't be retiring it for a long time.

PRE-GAME:

CAKE:
In large bowl place margarine and oats. Pour boiling water into bowl over oat mixture. Stir once or twice and set aside for 20 minutes.
Combine remaining ingredients in separate bowl.
Pour flour mixture into oat mixture; combine thoroughly.
Pour into 9" x 12" pan and bake at 375 degrees for 40 minutes.

FROSTING:
Mix all frosting ingredients. Spread evenly over cake.
Broil until coconut begins to brown.

SNICKERS RICH CANDY BAR CAKE

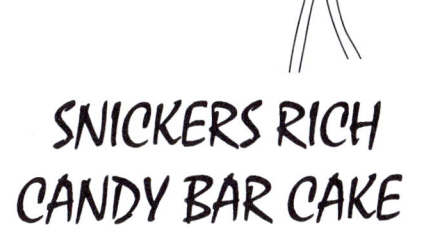

- 8 Snickers candy bars, regular size
- 2 sticks margarine
- 2 cups sugar
- 4 eggs, beaten
- 2-1/2 cups flour
- 1/2 teaspoon baking soda
- 1-1/2 cups buttermilk
- 1 cup pecans, chopped

FROSTING

- 2 to 2-1/2 cups sugar
- 1 (8-ounce) can evaporated milk
- 1 stick margarine
- 1 (6-ounce) package chocolate chips
- 1 cup marshmallow cream

PRE-GAME:

In a sauce pan melt one stick margarine and candy bars.
Cook over low heat stirring constantly. Set aside.
Cream sugar and 1 stick margarine in large bowl. Beat in eggs.
Sift flour and soda; add to creamed mixture alternating with buttermilk.
Add to candy mixture.
Stir in nuts and mix well.
Spray a 9" x 13" pan with non-stick spray. Flour lightly.
Pour mixture into pan.
Bake at 325 degrees for 1 hour 10 minutes.

FROSTING:
Combine remaining sugar, milk and margarine in a sauce pan. Cook to soft ball stage, stirring frequently. Remove from heat and add chocolate chips and marshmallow cream. Cool slightly. Beat until thick and spread over cake.

Yield: 14-16 servings

Note: You may substitute Milky Way Bars for Snickers, or mix the two.

This cake is incredibly rich, not unlike some of the multi-million dollar players in the NFL.
Randall Cunningham
7 years
$17.94 million
Barry Sanders
5 years
$6.1 million
Troy Aikman
6 years
$11.037 million

APRICOT CHOCOLATE BOMBE

4 eggs, extra large
1/3 cup sugar
3/4 cup oil
1 cup apricot nectar
1 package chocolate cake
  mix with pudding

FROSTING
4 tablespoons butter
1 (12-ounce) package semi-sweet
  chocolate chips
6 tablespoons milk
2 teaspoons vanilla
2 cups powdered sugar
1/2-3/4 cup walnuts, chopped

PRE-GAME:
In large bowl beat eggs well. Add sugar, oil, apricot nectar (shake to distribute pulp) and cake mix. Mix well after each addition. Spray bundt cake pan with non-stick oil. Pour mixture into pan. Bake at 350 degrees for 40-45 minutes or until toothpick comes out clean. Let cake sit no more than 5 minutes before unmolding. Frost immediately. Sprinkle with nuts.
Place cake in refrigerator until frosting is hard.

FROSTING: Melt butter in double boiler. Add chocolate chips, milk and vanilla. Remove from heat and combine with powdered sugar, mixing well.

THE BOMB
A long, forward pass thrown for substantial yardage is called a bomb. Some legendary quarterbacks (besides those already mentioned) are:
Terry Bradshaw
John Brodie
Lenny Dawson
Bob Griese
Sonny Jurgenson
Bobby Layne
Roger Staubach
Bart Starr
Danny White
Among wide receivers leaving their marks on the game were:
Lance Alworth
Fred Biletnikoff
Lynn Swann
Paul Warfield

SNOWBALL CAKE

2 envelopes unflavored gelatin
4 tablespoons cold water
Juice of 1 lemon
1 cup boiling water
1 cup sugar

1 (20-ounce) can crushed pineapple,
  drained
1 large (16-ounce) angel food cake
3 envelopes whipped topping mix
1 cup coconut, shredded

PRE-GAME:
Dissolve gelatin in cold water. Add lemon, boiling water, sugar and pineapple. Chill until slightly thickened.
Cut or tear cake into bite-size pieces. Place half the cake pieces in 9" x 13" pan.
Mix 3 envelopes whipped topping mix according to package directions. Add 2/3 of whipped mixture to gelatin.
Pour half of gelatin mixture over cake pieces. Top with remaining cake and gelatin mixture. Mix 1/2 cup coconut with remaining 1/3 whipped topping and spread on cake.
Sprinkle with remaining coconut and chill at least 1 hour.

Note: This cake freezes well.

EVERYBODY'S FAVORITE COOKIE SHEET CAKE

2 cups flour
2 cups sugar
1/2 teaspoon salt
2 sticks margarine
1 cup water

3 tablespoons cocoa
2 eggs, beaten
1 teaspoon soda
1/2 cup buttermilk
1 teaspoon vanilla

FROSTING

1 stick margarine
3 tablespoons cocoa

3 tablespoons milk

TOPPING

1 box powdered sugar
1 teaspoon vanilla

1 cup walnuts, chopped

PRE-GAME:

Place flour, sugar and salt in bowl.
Melt margarine, water and cocoa in saucepan.
When melted, pour over flour mixture.
Mix eggs, soda, buttermilk and vanilla. Add to flour and mix well.
Pour onto greased and floured cookie sheet or jelly-roll pan.
Bake at 350 degrees for 20 minutes.

FROSTING: Heat margarine in saucepan. Add cocoa and milk; mix.

TOPPING: Place powdered sugar, vanilla and nuts in medium-size bowl. Pour heated frosting into bowl with topping. Frost cake with this mixture after removing cake from oven.

JOE MONTANA
Joe Montana is practically a record book himself. He has quarterbacked the San Francisco 49ers to 4 Super Bowl Championships (1982, 1985, 1989, 1990). Montana is considered by many to be the player of the decade.

BEST EVER PECAN PIE

1 stick butter
1 cup light corn syrup
1 cup sugar
3 eggs, beaten
1/2 teaspoon lemon juice
1 teaspoon vanilla
1/8 teaspoon salt
1 cup pecans, chopped
8" or 9" unbaked pie shell

PRE-GAME:
Brown butter in saucepan until golden brown. Don't let it burn; cool. Place all other remaining ingredients in order in separate bowl; stir. Stir browned butter into bowl until well blended.
Pour into unbaked pie shell and bake at 425 degrees for 10 minutes. Lower temperature to 325 degrees and bake for 40 minutes or until knife inserted halfway between outside and center of filling comes out clean. Cool.

FRANK GIFFORD
Frank Gifford played for the New York Giants as a halfback. Gifford excelled throughout his football career, leading the Giants to six divisional championships. Later he joined ABC-TV as a sportscaster. Throughout his career, Frank Gifford has demonstrated professionalism and class. He has been the most enduring of the Monday Night football commentators.

This pie is a classic too! It's the best of the best!

BANANAS FOSTER TORTE

TORTE

4 egg whites
1-1/3 cups sugar
1-1/3 teaspoons baking powder
1 teaspoon vanilla
16 soda crackers, crushed
1 cup walnuts, chopped

FILLING

4 tablespoons butter
1 cup dark brown sugar
4 bananas, sliced
Banana liqueur
4 ounces light rum

TOPPING

1 cup whipping cream, whipped
1 teaspoon vanilla
1 tablespoon sugar

PRE-GAME:
Beat egg whites until stiff.
Sift sugar and baking powder together and fold into egg whites.
Add vanilla, crackers and walnuts, stirring after each addition.
Bake at 350 degrees in greased 8-9" pan or two cake pans. Cool.

FILLING: In saucepan melt butter. Stir in brown sugar. When well mixed add bananas. Add banana liqueur and light rum. Turn mixture coating bananas well.

TOPPING:
Whip cream and vanilla. Add sugar and whip until creamy, not grainy. Refrigerate.

SECOND-QUARTER
Assemble torte by layering bananas and whipped cream on top of the torte. Repeat layers. Top with whipped cream and chopped walnuts. Refrigerate until ready to serve.

FRAN TARKENTON
One of the most enjoyable quarterbacks to watch was Fran Tarkenton of the Minnesota Vikings and later the New York Giants.

Many an afternoon Tarkenton would be zig-zagging across the field scrambling to find an eligible receiver or added yardage on his own.

BERRY AND CITRUS TORTE

FILLING

3 bananas, sliced
2 oranges, peeled and sliced
3 kiwis, sliced

1 cup raspberries or sliced strawberries
1/2 cup Grand Mariner
2 tablespoons sugar

TORTE

1 ready-made pound cake

FROSTING

4 egg whites
2-1/2 cups whipping cream, chilled

1 cup powdered sugar
1/2 cup toasted slivered almonds

PRE-GAME:
Peel fruit and slice 1/4" thick.
Mix Grand Mariner and sugar, pour over fruit; cover and refrigerate.
TORTE: Slice pound cake into 3 lengthwise sections.
FROSTING: Beat 4 egg whites until stiff; set aside. In separate bowl, beat cream until thick. Add sugar and beat until soft peaks form. Fold in whites; refrigerate until ready to frost.

SECOND-QUARTER
Layer cake on a plate; frost, sprinkle with 1/3 of the fruit and sprinkle with nuts. Repeat for two more layers. Refrigerate.

Yield: 8 servings

RAYMOND BERRY
Raymond Berry was instrumental in the 1958 sudden-death win by the Baltimore Colts. Berry, a wide receiver, caught 3 Unitas passes for 62 yards helping set up the 20-yard Steve Myhra field goal.

FEARSOME FOURSOME PISTACHIO FOUR-LAYERED DESSERT

1 cup margarine
1-1/4 cups flour
1/2 cup walnuts
1 (8-ounce) package cream cheese, softened
1 cup powdered sugar
1 (12-ounce) container non-dairy whipped topping
2 small packages instant pistachio pudding
3 cups cold milk

TOPPING

Non-dairy whipped topping or 1 cup whipping cream, whipped
1/4 cup or more walnuts, chopped

PRE-GAME:

Mix margarine, flour, and walnuts; pat into 9" x 12" pan.
Bake 15 minutes at 350 degrees; cool.
Mix cream cheese, powdered sugar and whipped topping until smooth. Spread over crumb crust and chill.
Mix pudding and milk until thick; pour over first 2 layers.
Top with remaining whipped topping or whipped cream; sprinkle with walnuts. Refrigerate.

During the 1960s any team playing the Los Angeles Rams had to contend with their talented offensive line. The unit consisted of Merlin Olsen, Deacon Jones, Lamar Lundy and Roosevelt Grier. Deacon Jones earned another nickname, the "Secretary of Defense." He is also credited with the term "sack" (the quarterback). Merlin Olsen has been a winner on and off the field as an actor or announcer.

COLD ORANGE CRUSH SOUFFLE

2 envelopes unflavored gelatin
1 cup orange juice
6 eggs, separated
Rind, 1 orange, grated
Rind, 1 lemon, grated
1/4 cup lemon juice
2 cups sugar
3/4 teaspoon salt
2-1/2 cups whipping cream

PRE-GAME:

Sprinkle gelatin over 1/2 cup orange juice; set aside.
In saucepan mix egg yolks, orange and lemon rinds, 1/2 cup orange juice, lemon juice, 1-1/4 cups sugar and 3/4 teaspoon salt. Stir constantly over low heat until mixture thickens and coats a spoon. Remove from heat.
Stir in gelatin mixture until dissolved. Refrigerate 30-40 minutes until mixture mounds slightly when dropped from spoon (don't let it set). Beat egg whites until they hold soft peaks. Beat in remaining sugar. Beat until stiff.
Whip 2 cups whipping cream until stiff. Fold whites and whipped cream into chilled orange mixture.
Pour into 2-quart souffle dish. Seal with plastic wrap. Refrigerate overnight.
Garnish with remaining whipped cream, candied violets or grated chocolate.

JOHN ELWAY
John Elway is the talented quarterback of the "Orange Crush" team—the Denver Broncos. He holds the career record for his team in passing yards and passing touchdowns.

MILLION DOLLAR BACKFIELD SHREDDED APPLE PIE

1 pie crust (Processor pastry dough or traditional pie crust recipe) See p. 154

FILLING

3/4 cup sugar with zest of 2 lemons
3 Granny Smith apples, shredded
1 teaspoon cinnamon
Dash nutmeg

TOPPING

1/4 cup flour
1/3 cup dark brown sugar
5 tablespoons cold butter, sliced
1/2 cup walnuts (or more), chopped

PRE-GAME:

In food processor, mix lemon and sugar. Set aside.
Core but do not peel apples. Shred apples in processor and toss with lemon sugar. Set aside.

TOPPING: Process all ingredients together into crumb mixture with knife blade of food processor.
Grease tart or quiche pan lightly with non-stick spray and dust with flour. Place rolled-out pastry in pan.
Pre-cook pastry shell. Bake at 400 degrees 5-10 minutes.
When pastry is cool, fill with apple mixture and sprinkle on topping.
Bake at 375 degrees about 40 minutes or until done.

HALF-TIME:

Warm slightly before serving.

Serving suggestions: Serve with ice cream, whipped topping or ambrosia cream.

In the early 60's the San Francisco 49ers had some impressive players, namely Y.A. Tittle (quarterback), Hugh McElhenny (halfback), Joe Perry (fullback), and John Henry Johnson (fullback). They earned the nickname of the "Million Dollar Backfield."

BRANDY ALEXANDER PIE

2 prepared Graham Cracker Pie shells
1 envelope unflavored gelatin
1/2 cup water
2/3 cup sugar
1/8 teaspoon salt
3 eggs, separated
1/3 cup brandy
1/3 cup dark Creme de Cacao
1 cup heavy cream, whipped, for filling
1 cup heavy cream, whipped, for topping

PRE-GAME:
Sprinkle gelatin over cold water in saucepan to dissolve.
Add 1/3 cup sugar and salt.
Whisk egg yolks and add to saucepan.
Stir over low heat to thicken. Do not let boil.
Remove from heat and add liquor. Place saucepan in refrigerator up to one hour to cool.
Beat egg whites until stiff and add remaining sugar.
Beat 1 cup whipping cream.
Beat liquid in saucepan and fold in whipped cream and then egg whites.
Pour into pie shells and refrigerate for an hour until the pie sets up.
Top with whipping cream.

JOHN RIGGINS
Too bad John Riggins is retired from the game—he could always be counted on for needed yardage. As a fullback for the Washington Redskins his exploits on and off the field were legendary.

KING COCONUT CUSTARD PIE

COCONUT GRAHAM CRACKER CRUST

1 cup graham cracker crumbs
3/4 cup flaked coconut
2 tablespoons sugar
1 tablespoon honey
1/4 cup margarine, melted

FILLING

4 eggs
1/2 cup sugar
1/4 teaspoon salt
1 teaspoon vanilla
2-1/2 cups milk, scalded

TOPPING

1/4 cup brown sugar
2 tablespoons butter
1/2 cup coconut

PRE-GAME:
COCONUT CRUST:
In small bowl combine cracker crumbs with coconut, sugar and honey. Mix well. Stir in melted margarine. Press mixture firmly into bottom and sides of 9" pie pan. Bake at 375 degrees for 10 minutes or until lightly browned.

FILLING: (Preheat oven to 400 degrees.)
Beat eggs slightly. Stir in sugar, salt and vanilla.
Scald milk (heat milk until film covers pan).
Gradually add to egg mixture.
Cool thoroughly before filling.
Pour into chilled shell.
Bake at 400 degrees for 25-30 minutes or until knife inserted comes out clean. Cool.

SECOND QUARTER:
At the two-minute warning, before the *Half*: melt butter and brown sugar. Mix with coconut. Sprinkle mixture atop filling. Broil 3"-4" from heat for 2-4 minutes until browned.

HUGH McELHENNY
Hugh McElhenny could break away from pursuers by running from sideline to sideline downfield. This feat earned him the nickname, "The King." Some fans of the 1950s and 60s call this Hall of Famer and former San Francisco 49er the greatest runner of all time.

BOURBON AND WALNUT PIE

1 (9-inch) unbaked pie shell
4 eggs, beaten
1/2 cup butter, melted and cooled
1 cup light corn syrup
1/2 cup sugar
1/2 cup brown sugar, packed
1/4 cup bourbon
1 teaspoon vanilla
1 cup chopped walnuts
1/2 cup semi-sweet chocolate chips
Whipped cream, optional

PRE-GAME:

Stir eggs, butter and corn syrup together. Add sugars and mix well.
Add bourbon, vanilla and walnuts.
Sprinkle chocolate chips evenly over bottom of pie shell.
Carefully add egg mixture.
Bake at 350 degrees 45-55 minutes.
Serve with whipped cream.

Yield: 6-8 servings

Note: Substitute peppermint schnapps for bourbon, if desired.

RUNNING BACKS

Talented running backs provide fans with thrilling performances of speed and agility each week. The following running backs were among the best:
Marcus Allen
Alan Ameche
Earl Campbell
Billy Cannon
Tony Dorsett
Walt Garrison
Franco Harris
Calvin Hill
Jim Kiick
Lawrence McCutcheon
Gale Sayers.

KEY LIME PIE

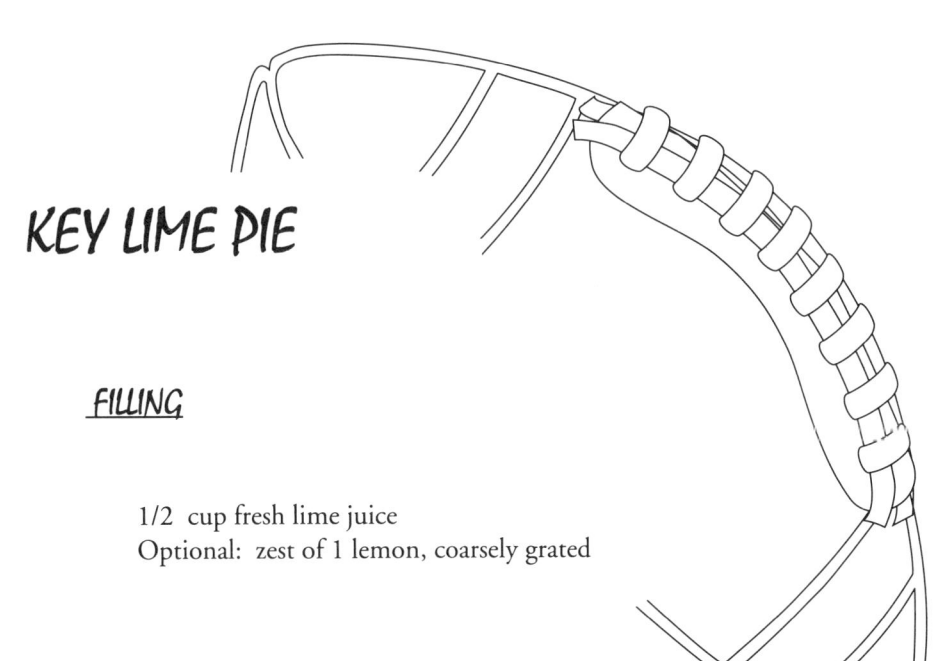

1 baked pie shell

FILLING

4 egg yolks
1 can sweetened condensed milk
1/2 cup fresh lime juice
Optional: zest of 1 lemon, coarsely grated

MERINGUE

3 egg whites
1/4 teaspoon cream of tartar
1/2 teaspoon vanilla
6 tablespoons superfine sugar

PRE-GAME:

FILLING:
Beat egg yolks until thick and lemon-colored. Add milk and blend. Add lime juice slowly. Mix in lemon zest. Pour into cool pie shell.

MERINGUE: Beat egg whites until foamy; add cream of tartar and beat until fluffy. Gradually beat in sugar; add vanilla.
Spread meringue over pie filling.
Bake until brown at 300 degrees.
Chill before serving.

LARRY CZONKA
Key lime means Florida and Florida means football. In the early '70's, the Miami Dolphins dominated the game. Larry Czonka contributed to their 1972 undefeated 14-0 season and Miami's consecutive wins in Super Bowl VII and VIII.

PEANUTTIEST PEANUT BUTTER DOUBLE RICH PIE

PIE SHELL

5 tablespoons margarine, melted
5 tablespoons peanut butter
22 (single-square) graham crackers, crushed
1/2 cup unsalted peanuts, chopped

PIE FILLING

1 (8-ounce) package cream cheese
1 cup superfine sugar
1 cup creamy peanut butter
1-1/2 cups whipping cream
1-1/2 teaspoons vanilla

TOPPING

4 ounces semi-sweet dark chocolate
2 tablespoons butter
1 tablespoon oil
1/4 cup peanuts, chopped

PRE-GAME:

PIE SHELL: Melt margarine and peanut butter. Add graham crackers and mix with fork. Add peanuts. Press in bottom and on sides of 10" pie pan. Bake at 375 degrees for 6-8 minutes. Cool.

PIE FILLING:
Beat cream cheese until fluffy. Slowly add sugar and continue to beat. Gradually add peanut butter, beating on low speed and scrap bowl. In separate bowl beat whipping cream until stiff, add vanilla. Beat about 1/3 of whipped cream into peanut butter mixture. Fold in remaining whipped cream.
Spread mixture into pie shell and chill at least one hour.

PIE TOPPING:
Melt grated chocolate with butter and oil in double boiler. Spread on top of pie filling. Chill. Garnish with chopped peanuts.

FIRST QUARTER:

Chill pie in refrigerator until *Half-Time.*

JIM PLUNKETT
KEN STABLER

Jim Plunkett served as quarterback for the Oakland (now L.A.) Raiders. His 80-yard bomb to Kenny King was the longest pass play in Super Bowl history.

Another Raider quarterback was the colorful Ken Stabler, 1970-79. Stabler, nicknamed the Snake, holds the team record for career passing yards and touchdowns.

BANANA SPLIT THE UPRIGHTS PIZZA PIE DESSERT

- 1 package refrigerator sugar cookie dough
- 1 (8-ounce) package cream cheese
- 1/3 cup sugar
- 1 tablespoon fruit juice
- 2 cups mandarin oranges, well-drained
- 1 (8-ounce) can chunk pineapple, well-drained
- 6 strawberries, sliced
- 3 bananas, sliced
- Lemon juice
- Apricot preserves or orange marmalade
- 1/2 cup pecans, chopped
- 1/2 cup shredded coconut
- Vanilla ice cream and/or whipped topping (optional)

PRE-GAME:

Place sliced cookie dough on pizza pan close enough so the dough runs together when baked. Bake at 350 degrees until golden brown. Cool.
Cream sugar, fruit juice and cream cheese together.
Spread over crust. Arrange fruit evenly around the crust or in rows.
Heat preserves or marmalade and spoon over top.
Sprinkle with pecans and coconut.

HALF-TIME:

Spoon ice cream over nuts. Smooth on top.
Cover with whipped topping.
Slice and serve.

Yield: 8 servings

TOM DEMPSEY
This is a dessert to celebrate the feat performed by Tom Dempsey of the New Orleans Saints on November 8, 1970. The Lions scored with 11 seconds to go in the game. Quarterback Al Dodd got the Saints to their 45-yard line. With two seconds left on the clock, Tom Dempsey was called in to kick a 63-yard field goal. As the ball split the uprights the Saints, moved ahead of the Lions 19-17, and Dempsey's accomplishment moved into the record books.

PIE SHELLS

PIE CRUST USING A FOOD PROCESSOR

1-2/3 cup unbleached
    all-purpose flour (pre-sifted)
1/4 teaspoon salt
1/2 cup sweet butter

1/4 cup cold water
1 egg yolk
1 tablespoon oil

PRE-GAME:

Place flour, salt and butter in food processor. Turn machine off and on until mixture is coarse. While machine is on add cold water, egg yolk and oil. The mixture will become ball-shaped.
Place in refrigerator for at least one half hour.
Roll out on floured board or between sheets of floured wax paper.
To transfer pastry, roll it over a rolling pin; unroll pastry over pie plate, fitting loosely onto bottom and sides.

Note: Bake according to filling instructions

TRADITIONAL PIE CRUST (without a food processor)

Single Crust:

1-1/2 cups sifted all-purpose flour
1/2 teaspoon salt
1/2 cup shortening
4-5 tablespoons cold water

Double Crust:

2 cups sifted all purpose flour
1 teaspoon salt
2/3 cup shortening
5-7 tablespoons cold water

PRE-GAME:

Sift together flour and salt. Cut in shortening with pastry blender until pieces are pea-sized. Sprinkle 1 tablespoon water over part of mixture. Gently toss with a fork; push to one side of bowl.
Sprinkle 1 tablespoon water over dry part; mix lightly; push to moistened part at side. Repeat until all dough is moist.
Gather dough with fingers; form into a ball. (Divide for a two-crust pie.)
On lightly floured surface, flatten ball slightly and roll to 1/8" thickness.
If edges split, pinch together. Always roll spoke-fashion--from center to edge. Transfer to pie plate by folding dough over rolling pin.
Double-crust pie: Fit the lower crust in pie plate. Add filling.
Place upper crust on top.
Slash upper crust with your own design. Trim crusts. Pinch edges.
Bake according to directions for filling.

SUBSTITUTION

Unlimited substitution is permitted. Players may be sent onto the field of play, however only when the ball is dead.

Do you substitute ready made pie shells for the real thing? If you haven't been successful at making pie crusts in the past, try using your food processor. It's easy and quick.

FIELD SUPPORT SPECIAL DISHES

It takes more than 22 members of the starting line-up to make a game exciting. From the personalities in the broadcast booth to the coaches pacing along the sidelines—each brings expertise to an NFL game.

The same principle works in meal preparation. Special dishes are needed to support or enliven entrees. After all, can you imagine fajitas without salsa or hamburgers without baked beans? I can't. These dishes enhance your entrees.

REFEREE'S RICE

1-1/2 cups fresh mushrooms
2 teaspoons margarine or olive oil
2 cups long grain rice, uncooked
2 cubes butter or margarine
1 onion, chopped

1 bell pepper, chopped
1 teaspoon salt
2 cups onion soup
2 cups water

PRE-GAME:
Slice and saute mushrooms in margarine or olive oil.
Place following 5 ingredients in pan: rice, butter/margarine, bell pepper, onion and salt; brown lightly. Add mushrooms, soup and water. Place in 3-quart baking dish.
Bake at 350 degrees for 1 hour, 15 minutes.

SECOND QUARTER:
Reheat rice in oven on low temperature.

THE REFEREE
The referee is actually one of seven officials on the field. He lines up behind the offensive backfield. The umpire, head linesman, field judge, back judge, line judge and side judge are under the command of the referee.

SPECIAL TEAMS' SPICY RICE

6 cups cooked rice
2 pints sour cream
1 (12-ounce) can diced green chiles

1 pound Monterey Jack cheese, shredded
1/2 to 1 cup Parmesan cheese

PRE-GAME:
Spread half the cooked rice in a 13" x 9" pan.
Spread 1 pint sour cream over rice; place half the chiles evenly over sour cream. Top with shredded cheese. Repeat layers.
Top with Parmesan cheese.

SECOND QUARTER:
Bake at 350 degrees, 25-30 minutes.

Yield: 10 servings

SPECIAL TEAMS
Special teams, needed for specific duties, serve on the kickoff, kickoff return, punt, punt return and field goal units.

COACH POTATOES GORGONZOLA

6 large russet potatoes, well scrubbed
1/2 teaspoon thyme
1/2 teaspoon basil
1/2 teaspoon oregano
1/2 teaspoon salt
1/2 teaspoon seasoning salt
1/2 teaspoon pepper
1/4 teaspoon cayenne
1/2 teaspoon chili powder
1-1/2 cups flour
2 eggs
1/3 cup milk
1/4 cup oil
1/2 pound Gorgonzola cheese, crumbled

PRE-GAME:
Slice potatoes into fourths lengthwise.
Mix seasonings and flour.
Mix eggs with milk.
Dip potato wedges into milk mixture and dust with seasoned flour.
Place on a pastry sheet.
Drizzle with oil.

SECOND QUARTER:
Place potatoes in oven at beginning of quarter.
Bake at 425 degrees for 20-25 minutes or until browned and tender.
Sprinkle cheese over wedges. Heat until melted.

HALF-TIME:
Serve potatoes hot.

Yield: 24 potato wedges

The opposite of "couch potatoes" are the hard working individuals who guide your favorite team(s). Some of my favorite coaches of yesterday and today are:
George Allen
Paul Brown
Tom Flores
Joe Gibbs
Bud Grant
Chuck Knox
Tom Landry
Vince Lombardi
John Madden
Chuck Noll
Don Shula.

COMMON TATERS

1 medium sized russet potato per fan
oil

Seasoning salt
Seasoned pepper

PRE-GAME:
Scrub potatoes and prick with a fork. Rub skins with oil and place on a cookie sheet. Sprinkle seasoning salt and pepper on top each potato. Bake at 400 degrees for 1 to 1-1/2 hours or until done.

SECOND QUARTER:
Reheat baked potatoes in the oven until hot. Don't overcook. The ideal would be to have the baked potatoes started before the *First Quarter* so they're ready by *Half-Time*.

High above the playing field, the broadcast teams explain the game of football via radio or television. Over the years some of my favorite commentators on NFL games have been: Frank Gifford, John Madden, Don Meredith and Merlin Olsen. Yes, even Howard Cosell, left his mark.

POTATO TOPPINGS

Butter
Sour cream
Grated cheese
Diced black olives
Cottage cheese

Cubed ham
Bacon bits
Mushrooms
Whole kernel corn
Broccoli

Plan a vegetable appetizer and steam any remaining vegetables for a potato topping.

Place toppings in separate bowls.

HALF-TIME:
Slice potatoes in half or just through the center.
Serve whole or in halves.

T.V. CREW-TONS
(Croutons)

1 loaf bread—buttermilk, sourdough, etc.
   (Whatever is in the freezer, non-preservative bread works best)
1 cube margarine
Choice of seasonings:
   Garlic • Rosemary • Thyme • Cayenne pepper
   Chervil • Tarragon

PRE-GAME:
Pre-heat oven to 350 degrees.
Melt margarine in a 12" x 18" cake pan.
Slice bread into cubes while frozen; cut-off crusts.*
Distribute evenly in pan.
Cubes will need to be turned in 1-2 minutes.
Halfway through the heating, add seasoning(s).
Cooking time is approximately 7-8 minutes each side.
May be stored in plastic containers up to 3 months.

*Place crusts in food processor; crumble for bread crumbs.

PRESS BOX BAKED BEANS

1 large can pork and beans
1 cup ketchup
1 cup brown sugar
2 tablespoon prepared mustard
1 large onion, chopped
1 green bell pepper, chopped
8 slices bacon

PRE-GAME:
Mix ingredients in a large casserole.
Lay strips of bacon across top.
Bake at 350 degrees for 4 hours.

FIRST QUARTER:
If it has already baked at least four hours, either the day ahead or earlier in the day, simply reheat on low temperature.

PRESS BOX
Members of the working press record the game's action for the print media in this enclosure. Assistant coaches may coordinate play calling from this vantage point too.

GROUNDSKEEPERS GRIDIRON GRITS

3-1/2 cups water
1-1/2 cups milk
1 teaspoon salt
1-1/4 cups quick grits, uncooked
1 stick margarine
1 (5-ounce) jar sharp pasturized process cheese spread
12 ounces sharp cheddar cheese, grated
1 tablespoon Worcestershire sauce
2 teaspoons garlic spread
1/4 cup fresh chives, snipped
1/2 teaspoon cayenne pepper
Paprika

PRE-GAME:

In a saucepan, bring water, milk and salt to boil. Add grits, reduce heat and cook until done, stirring occasionally. Add margarine, cheese, Worcestershire, garlic spread, chives and cayenne pepper. Stir until cheese is melted. Place in 3-quart casserole. Dust with paprika.

SECOND QUARTER:

Bake for 15-20 minutes in 350-degree oven.

Yield: 12 servings

CHAIN CREW ZUCCHINI CRUST CASSEROLE

1-1/2 cups cooked brown rice
1 egg
3/4 cup cheddar cheese, shredded
1 pound bacon, cooked
2 large onions, chopped

14 pieces zucchini, sliced 1/2" thick
Garlic powder or salt
Parmesan cheese

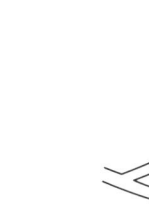

PRE-GAME:
Mix rice, egg and cheese. Pat into 8" square pan.
Cook bacon, drain. Cut into 1" pieces.
Saute chopped onions in bacon fat. Drain.
Cook zucchini about 5 minutes (no longer) and drain well.
Place zucchini, onions and bacon over rice crust.
Sprinkle with a garlic salt or powder (optional).
Cover with approximately 1/4" Parmesan cheese.
Bake at 350 degrees for 30 minutes.

SECOND QUARTER:
Reheat at 300 degrees approximately 10 minutes before *Half-Time.*

Yield: 8-10 servings

CHAIN CREW
A boxman and two rodmen handle the first-down yardage equipment. The head linesman supervises these three members of the chain crew.

MILD FANS' SALSA

1 (28-ounce) can tomatoes
1 (8-ounce) can diced green chiles
3 tablespoons wine vinegar
3 tablespoons oil
Garlic salt
Freshly ground pepper
8 green onions, sliced
   (including 2" of green tops)
2 small cans sliced black olives

PRE-GAME:
Mix ingredients; store in jars. Refrigerate. Salsa will keep for several weeks. Serve at room temperature.

You've seen these fans in the stands. They're usually under control unless a particularly grievous error is called against their team. They reluctantly participate in the "wave", booing or excessive displays of emotion.

WILD FANS SALSA

- 2 pounds ripe tomatoes, peeled, remove seeds, finely chop
- 2 bell peppers, de-rib, remove seeds, finely chop
- 2 small onions, finely chop
- 2-4 jalapeño peppers, remove seeds, finely chop
- 4 tablespoons fresh lime juice
- 4 tablespoons chopped cilantro
- 1/2 teaspoon salt

PRE-GAME:
Mix ingredients; store in jars. Refrigerate. Serve salsa however, at room temperature.

CHILI PEPPERS

Chili Peppers—use according to the taste of the fans. Take care in handling fresh or dried chiles. Use plastic gloves and/or wash your hands before touching skin or eyes.

Anaheim—Although they are usually green in color, some may be red. They are mild in flavor and are often used in canned chiles.

Jalapeños—These mild to very hot chiles have rounded tips. They are usually green, ripening to mottled green and orange.

Yellow wax—Yellow to yellow-orange in color, these chiles have a taste similar to bell peppers. They may range from mild to somewhat hot.

Serranos—Although the smallest in size they carry the most fire. Their red color serves as a warning signal although some may be green prior to ripening. They range from mildly hot to firecracker hot.

Wild fans are easily provoked by any referee's whistle or the belief of unfair advantage given to their opponent. These zealots may be identified by the following characteristics: (a) apparel sporting their team's name, (b) banner-waving, (c) jockeying for position in front of television cameras, (d) standing during most plays of the game and (e) the ability for their voice to carry into the next county. These rabid fans usually have season tickets right next to yours.

FOOTBALL PARTY MENUS

Catching the ball deep and running it back for a touchdown—the dream of every football player. The recipes in FUMBLE FREE: A FOOTBALL COOKBOOK will bring their own record-setting compliments.

Draft friends to bring dishes. Follow menus precisely or become a free-agent searching for suitable dishes from the other menu teams.

The secret to successful party food planning is combining compatible dishes as well as judging the quantity needed.

Drafting players for a team works the same way—anticipating talent and need.

Draft: A system to achieve fairness in the selection of suitable college players to NFL teams. Allows for teams with the worst won-loss record to select first unless that privilege has been traded.

Free-Agent: A player not drafted by an NFL team. Also any player is eligible to negotiate with another team if his contract has lapsed. A player may also come to training camp by invitation or application.

GAME 1

Entree: Roughing the Kicker Kabobs

Appetizer: Hot Crab Dip   Layered Mexican Dip

Salad: Avocado-Citrus Salad

Bread: Lateral Pass Mozzarella Loaf

Dessert: Fearsome Foursome Four-Layered Dessert or Old Fashioned Oatmeal Cake

GAME 2

Entree: Rushing the Passer Roast Beef Pasta

Appetizer: Sesame Honey Chicken   Clam Spread

Salad: Monterey Jack Melange Salad

Bread: Onside Kick Bread Sticks

Extra: Antipasta Bean Salad

Dessert: Chocolate Chip Bars   Peanuttiest Peanut Butter Pie

GAME 3

Entree: Safety Savory Vegetable Soup and/or Offensive Players' Onion Soup

Appetizer: Chili Con Quesa   Steak Tartare

Salad: Peas and Cashew Crunch Salad

Bread: Off-Setting Penalties Onion Herb Bread

Dessert: Berry and Citrus Torte   Peanut Butter Cookies   Quick Cookies

GAME 4

Entree: Linebacker Basil Burgers

Appetizer: Oyster Fritters   Vegetable Squares

Salad: Sour Cream Potato Salad or Pepper and Pickle Pasta

Bread: Hamburger Buns

Extra   Press Box Baked Beans

Dessert: Bourbon and Walnut Pie   Apple Praline Cake

GAME 5

Entree: Defensive Formation Beef Stroganoff

Appetizer: Eggplant and Whole Wheat Pita Crisps   Crab Puffs

Salad: Caesar Salad

Bread: Automatic First Down Automatic Honey Bread
    Fair Catch Cottage Cheese Beer Bread

Dessert: Million Dollar Backfield Shredded Apple Pie
    Memorable Chocolate Mousse Cake

GAME 6

Entree: Defensive Lineman Lasagna

Appetizer: Cheese, Olive and/or Parmesan Cheese Balls
    Undressed Shrimp

Salad: Romano, Romaine and Red Leaf Salad

Bread: Forward Pass Foccacio Bread

Dessert: A Lot of Lemon Bars   Gingersnap Bars

GAME 7

Entree: Quarterback Grilled or Barbecue Chicken

Appetizer: Crab Mold   Black-eyed Pea Dip   Dressed Shrimp

Salad: Tex-Mex Caesar Salad   Pasta/Sausage Salad

Bread: Unsportsmanlike Cheese Chili Bread

Dessert: Everybody's Favorite Cookie Sheet Cake,
King Custard Coconut Pie

GAME 8

Entree: Defensive Back Beef Bourguignon

Appetizer: 20-Yard Line Teriyaki Chicken Wings
Potato Pancakes Caviar

Salad: Aspic Salad   Broccoli-Cauliflower Salad

Bread: Personal Foul Gourmet French Bread

Dessert: German Chocolate Cream Cheese Brownies
Bananas Foster Torte

GAME 9

Entree: Tight End Chiladas—Chicken and/or Beefy

Appetizer: Reuben Dip   Caviar Mousse   Scrimmage Spinach

Salad: Red Tip Lettuce Salad with Vermouth Dressing

Bread: Throw a Block Bacon Cheese Bread

Extra: Defensive Tackle Tamale Pie

Dessert: B and B Million-Dollar Liqueur Cake
Rocky Road Brownies

GAME 10

Entree: Cornerback Chili

Appetizer: Avocado Crab   Blue Cheese Ball with Crackers

Salad: Mozzarella-Mushroom Salad

Bread: Clipping Corn Bread Squares

Dessert: Key Lime Pie   Pecan Chocolate Chip Cookies

GAME 11

Entree: Center Cheese Chowder

Appetizer: On the Numbers Nachos   Fruit and Peanutty Dip

Salad: Special Spinach Salad

Bread: Touchdown Rolls

Dessert: Double Chocolate Crumble Bars   Snowball Cake

GAME 12

Entree: Halfback Halibut or Guard au Gratin Baked Fish

Appetizer: Mexicali Sombrero Skins   Guacamole Dunk

Salad: Cabbage Crunch Salad or Three R's --Romaine, Raisin and Red Dressing Salad

Bread: Handoff Hearty Herb Bread

Extra: Referee's Rice

Dessert: Brandy Alexander Pie   M-M-M Monster Cookies   Orange Jewel Cookies

GAME 13

Entree: Free-Safety Seasoned Meatloaf

Appetizer: Taxi Squad Tortilla Pie   Dill Dip and Vegetables

Salad: Coliseum Coleslaw

Bread: Offside Onion Cake

Extra: Common Taters or Chain Crew
Zucchini Casserole

Dessert: Cold Orange Crush Souffle
Snicker's Rich Candy Bar Cake

GAME 14

Entree: Sack the Quarterback Salsa and Beef Fajitas

Appetizer: First and Ten Mussels   Stuffed Mushrooms

Salad: Vegetable Layered Salad

Bread: Free Kick Herb-Buttered French Bread

Extra: Special Teams' Spicy Rice

Dessert: Charter Caramel Cookies   Best Ever Pecan Pie

GAME 15

Entree: Wide Receiver's Wild Rice and Chicken Vol-au-Vent

Appetizer: Tex-Mex Beef Dip   Salmon Ball

Salad: Gruyere Salad and Vinaigrette

Bread: Pass Interference Pepper, Parmesan, Paprika Twists

Dessert: Apricot Chocolate Bombe
Banana Split the Uprights Pizza Pie Dessert

FUSSY FANS

Some football parties have an "adults-only" policy. If your football events include younger children you may wish to serve alternative entrees or kids' food. Consider serving children early or after the *First Quarter*—before they become FUSSY FANS.

TUNA NOODLE CASSEROLE

1 (6-ounce) package medium noodles
1 (14-ounce) can tuna
1/2 cup mayonnaise
1 cup celery, sliced
1/2 cup onion, chopped
1/4 cup bell pepper, diced
1/4 cup pimiento
1/2 teaspoon salt
1 can cream of celery soup
1/2 cup milk
1 (small) can sliced water chestnuts
2 eggs, hard-boiled, chopped
1/2 cup frozen peas, defrosted
1-2 teaspoons rosemary
1 cup sharp cheddar cheese, shredded
1/2 cup slivered almonds (optional)
Potato chips

PRE-GAME:
Cook noodles in boiling salted water until tender; drain.
Saute celery, onion and bell pepper in a small amount of oil until somewhat softened.
In a casserole mix all ingredients, except potato chips.

SECOND QUARTER:
Bake at 350 degrees for 15 minute; top with potato chips.
Bake 15 minutes more.

Yield: 5 servings

PARTY PIZZAS

6 English muffins
1 pound sharp cheese, grated
1/4 cup oil
6 green onions, chopped
1 (8-ounce) can tomato sauce
1 (4-ounce) can chopped green chiles
1/4 cup chopped ripe olives

PRE-GAME:
Slice muffins in half. Mix ingredients and spread on muffins.

SECOND QUARTER:
Bake at 350 degrees 15 minutes or until hot.
Serve whole or cut in wedges.

Note: Muffins may be frozen by placing each prepared muffin between sheets of waxed paper and storing in plastic bags or freezer wrap.

SPAGHETTI

1 onion, chopped
1 green pepper, chopped
1 pound ground beef
1 can tomato soup
1 can cream of mushroom soup
1 can water
1/2 pound cheddar cheese, grated
1/2 teaspoon Italian seasoning
1 (7-ounce) package spaghetti

PRE-GAME:
Saute onion and green pepper in oil. When limp, remove from skillet. Brown meat and drain. Add soups, water, onion, green pepper and meat to skillet. Simmer 30-40 minutes. Add cheese. When melted, mix ingredients with cooked spaghetti.

SECOND QUARTER:
Bake at 350 degrees 25-30 minutes or until "bubbly." Do not overcook.

Note: This is one casserole that tastes best when it hasn't been reheated.

BEEF AND BEANS CASSEROLE

1 pound hamburger
1/2 pound bacon, cut up
1 can pork and beans
1 can lima beans, drained
1 can kidney beans, drained
1 cup onion, chopped
1/2 cup ketchup
3/4 cup brown sugar
2 teaspoons vinegar
1 teaspoon mustard
1-1/2 teaspoons chili powder
1/2 cup chili sauce

PRE-GAME:
Brown hamburger and bacon, drain.
Mix all ingredients.
Top with chili sauce.

FIRST QUARTER:
Bake at 350 degrees for 40 minutes.

RED DOG
To blitz
(see page 45)
PINK DOG
Blitz by outside linebacker
HALFBACK DOG
Cornerback blitz

CORN DOGS

1 pound hot dogs
10 wooden sticks
1/2 cup flour
1/3 cup corn meal
1 tablespoon sugar
1 teaspoon dry mustard
1 teaspoon baking powder
1/2 teaspoon salt
1 tablespoon oil
1/2 cup milk
1 egg

PRE-GAME:
Dry hot dogs and insert stick into hot dog.
Mix remaining ingredients. Pour into a tall glass.
Coat hot dogs by placing each one in the glass of dough.
Drop coated hot dogs into 2 inches or more of hot oil (approximately 375 degrees).
It takes 3-4 minutes to brown. Drain on paper towels.

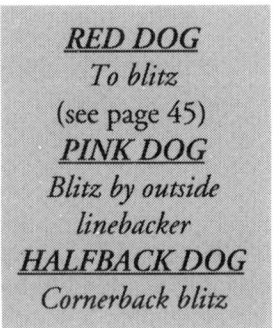

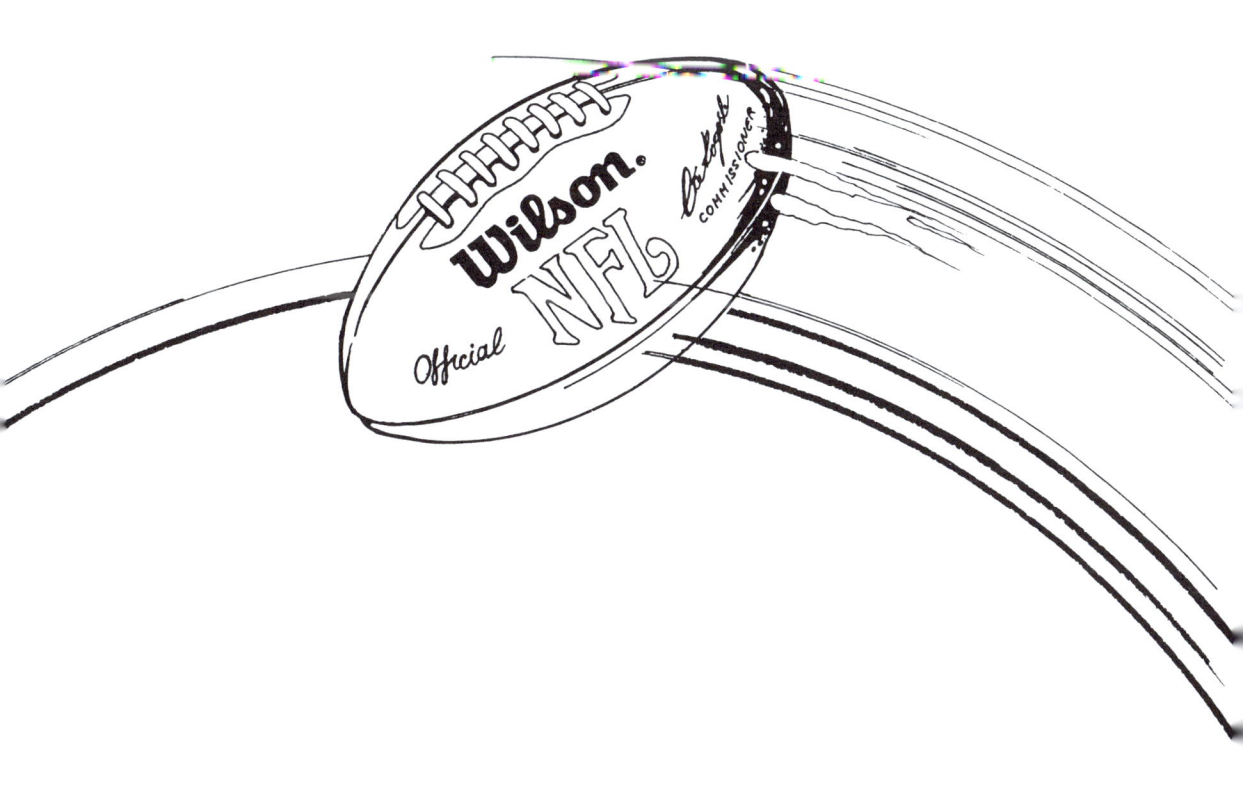

THE SUPER BOWL

173

SUPER BOWL RESULTS

1967	Green Bay	35	Kansas City	10
1968	Green Bay	33	Oakland	14
1969	N.Y. Jets	16	Baltimore	7
1970	Kansas City	23	Minnesota	7
1971	Baltimore	16	Dallas	13
1972	Dallas	24	Miami	3
1973	Miami	14	Washington	7
1974	Miami	24	Minnesota	7
1975	Pittsburgh	16	Minnesota	6
1976	Pittsburgh	21	Dallas	17
1977	Oakland	32	Minnesota	14
1978	Dallas	27	Denver	10
1979	Pittsburgh	35	Dallas	31
1980	Pittsburgh	31	Los Angeles	19
1981	Oakland	27	Philadelphia	10
1982	San Francisco	26	Cincinnati	21
1983	Washington	27	Miami	17
1984	L.A. Raiders	38	Washington	9
1985	San Francisco	38	Miami	16
1986	Chicago	46	New England	10
1987	N.Y. Giants	39	Denver	20
1988	Washington	42	Denver	10
1989	San Francisco	20	Cincinnati	16
1990	San Francisco	55	Denver	10
1991	N.Y. Giants	20	Buffalo	19
1992	_____	__	_____	__
1993	_____	__	_____	__
1994	_____	__	_____	__
1995	_____	__	_____	__
1996	_____	__	_____	__

FUTURE SUPER BOWLS
1992
Metrodome
Minneapolis, MN
January 26
1993
Rose Bowl, Pasadena, CA
1994
Atlanta, GA
1995
Miami, FL

SUPER BOWL MENU

Your Super Bowl Party begins with a pre-game brunch and some friendly betting on the outcome of the game. Choose any of these easy-to-prepare dishes for your Super Bowl day.

ALL-DAY MUNCHIES

Football Nuts and Bolts, Beer Nuts
or Trail Mix Popcorn

BRUNCH

Orange Juice, Bloody Marys, Champagne, Flavored Coffees

Instant Replay Fresh Fruit
Grapefruit, Oranges, Cantaloupe, Apples, Tangerines,
Bananas, Kiwi, Grapes and/or Pineapple

Pro Bowl Hawaiian Bread, Grapefruit Bread, Healthy
Muffins, Carmel and Pull-Apart Rolls

Superstar Brunch Casserole

HALF-TIME

Hall of Fame Ham or Football Hero Sandwich

Tangy Mustard

Super Bowl Ring

Countdown Curried Fruit

Wild Card Wild Rice and Sausage Casserole

Most Valuable Player Mocha Mint Cheesecake
"The Party's Over" Pina Colada Cake

FOOTBALL NUTS AND BOLTS

5 cups Wheat Chex
5 cups Corn Chex
5 cups Cheerios
5 cups pretzels

2 pounds mixed nuts
1 pound butter
6 tablespoons Worcestershire sauce
4 tablespoons garlic salt

PRE-GAME:
Melt butter, add Worcestershire and garlic salt. Mix well.
Pour over cereals and blend.
Bake in a 250 degree oven; turn every 15 minutes for 1 hour.

Note: A turkey roasting pan works best.

BEER NUTS

1 pound raw peanuts
1 cup sugar
1/2 cup water

PRE-GAME:
Boil ingredients until dry. Spread on cookie sheet; salt to taste.
Bake at 300 degrees for 30 minutes, stirring occasionally.

TRAIL MIX POPCORN

2 tablespoons margarine
1/4 cup honey
1 tablespoon lemon peel, grated
1/4 teaspoon cinnamon
2 quarts popcorn, plain, popped

1 cup raisins
1-1/2 cups dried apricots, chopped, or other dried fruit
1 cup unsalted peanuts

PRE-GAME:
Melt margarine in small saucepan; stir in honey, lemon peel and cinnamon.
Toss with popcorn.
Add remaining ingredients.

INSTANT REPLAY FRESH FRUIT

1 grapefruit, sectioned
2 oranges, sectioned
3 apples, sliced
Juice 1 lemon
2 tangerines, sectioned
3 bananas, sliced
3 kiwis, peeled and sliced
2 cups grapes
Cherry brandy, to taste

PRE-GAME:

Slice grapefruit and orange sections in half. Dip apples in lemon juice to preserve color. Mix fruit together, except grapes, with cherry brandy. Add grapes and mix. Refrigerate.
Use INSTANT REPLAY FRUIT, around SUPER BOWL RING, too.

INSTANT REPLAY
A limited instant replay system was approved in 1986. A replay official, in a replay booth, views the game from a live network feed, but he can not ocmmunicate with television personnel about which plays are to be shown. Many plays or fouls do not fall under the instant replay system and therefore it's called "limited instant replay." The belief is that on-field officials have the best view of most fouls.

PRO BOWL HAWAIIAN BREAD

3 cups all-purpose flour
2 cups sugar
1 teaspoon soda
1 teaspoon salt
1 teaspoon ground cinnamon
1/2 teaspoon nutmeg
3 eggs, beaten
1/2 cup melted butter or margarine
1 cup oil
2 teaspoons vanilla
1/2 teaspoon coconut flavoring
2 cups coconut (flaked or shredded)
2 cups mashed ripe bananas (the blacker the better)
1 (8-ounce) can crushed pineapple, drained
1 cup pecans, chopped

PRE-GAME:

Combine flour, sugar, soda, salt, cinnamon and nutmeg in large bowl.
Beat eggs in small bowl; add margarine, oil, vanilla and coconut flavoring; mix well. Add egg mixture to ingredients; stir until moistened.
Add bananas, pineapple, nuts and 1 cup coconut.
Spoon batter into 2 greased and floured 9" x 5" x 3" loaf pans.
Bake at 350 degrees for 50 minutes. Sprinkle 1 cup coconut on top and bake an additional 15 to 20 minutes (or until tooth pick comes out clean). Cover with foil the last 5-10 minutes if coconut is darkening too much.

PRO BOWL

After the Super Bowl selected players from the National Football Conference and the American Football Conference play in the Pro Bowl.

Since 1980 it has been held at Aloha Stadium, Honolulu, Hawaii.

PULL-APART CARAMEL BREAKFAST ROLLS

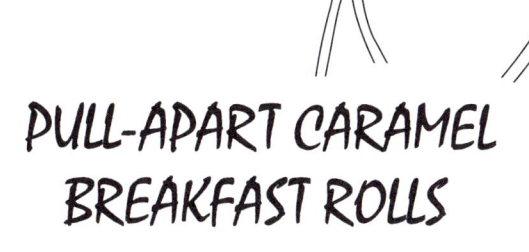

2   1 pound loaves frozen bread dough, thawed
1   cup brown sugar
1   (5.5 ounce) package regular vanilla pudding
1/2 cup margarine, melted
1/4 cup half and half
1/2 cup pecans, chopped

PRE-GAME:
Cut one loaf of dough into small pieces, place in greased 9" x 13" pan.
(A bundt pan may also be used.) Combine all ingredients except pecans.
Drizzle half this mixture over dough pieces with 1/4 cup nuts.
Repeat process for second loaf.
Cover. Refrigerate several hours or overnight.
Bake at 325 degrees for 50 minutes. While still warm, turn upside down.

GRAPEFRUIT NUT BREAD

2 cups flour
1 cup sugar
1 tablespoon baking powder
1 teaspoon salt
1/2 cup grapefruit peel, chopped
1 cup walnuts and/or pecans, chopped
1 egg, beaten
3/4 cup milk
1/4 cup melted butter or margarine
1/4 cup grapefruit juice

PRE-GAME:
Mix flour, sugar, baking powder and salt.
Add chopped grapefruit peel and nuts.
Combine egg, milk, butter and grapefruit juice in separate bowl.
Mix together and add to flour mixture.
Turn into greased 9" x 5" loaf pan. Bake at 350 degrees 1 hour.
Cool on a rack.
Slice and serve.

SUPERSTAR BRUNCH CASSEROLE

8 slices stale white bread without crusts
3/4 pound cheddar cheese, grated
1-1/2 pounds skinless sausages, cooked and sliced about 1/2" size
4 eggs
2-1/2 cups milk
3/4 teaspoon prepared mustard
1/4 cup dry vermouth
1 can cream of mushroom soup
1/2 pound mushrooms, sliced

PRE-GAME:
Grease bottom of 9-1/2" x 13" pan with non-stick spray.
Cube bread and place on bottom of pan.
Top with cheese. Mix eggs, milk, mustard and vermouth in bowl.
Pour evenly over top of casserole. Spread cream of mushroom soup over egg mixture. Bake at 350 degrees for 1 hour.
Top with sliced mushrooms and bake 5-10 minutes more.

Yield: 8-10 servings

EATING HEALTHY
1. Use unsaturated vegetable oils such as olive, corn, peanut, canola, safflower, sesame and soybean.
2. Limit saturated fat to less than 10 percent of total calories.
3. Eat less than 300 milligrams of cholesterol a day.
4. Choose skim milk and skim milk products. Decrease whole milk, evaporated and condensed milk.
5. Choose egg whites; decrease egg yolks.
6. Choose lean cuts of beef.
7. Remove skin from poultry.
8. Reduce the amount of salt by one-half.

HEALTHY MUFFINS

2-1/2 cups oat flour *
1-1/2 cups bran
2-1/2 teaspoons baking soda
1 cup oatmeal, whole rolled oats
2 teaspoons cinnamon
dash nutmeg
dash allspice
1/2 teaspoon salt or salt substitute
5-6 ripe bananas, pureed
1 cup low fat milk
1/4 cup molasses
1/4 cup honey
1/3 cup concentrated apple juice
1/4 cup raisins
1/4 cup pecans, chopped
1/4 cup dates, chopped
2 eggs or egg substitute

*If oat flour is unavailable, process oatmeal into a coarse flour texture.

PRE-GAME:
Mix all ingredientsr in bowl except eggs.
Beat eggs and fold into bowl.
Bake in greased muffin tins at 325 degrees 15-20 minutes or until done.

TANGY MUSTARD

1 package unflavored gelatin
3 tablespoons water
4 eggs, beaten
3/4 cup sugar
2 tablespoons dry mustard

3/4 cup vinegar
1/3 cup water
Salt (optional)
1 cup heavy cream, whipped

PRE-GAME:
Simmer water in bottom of a double boiler. In top of double boiler, dissolve gelatin in water. Add all ingredients except cream.
Cook until thick. Cool.
Fold in whipped cream. Spoon mixture into a mold. Chill until firm.

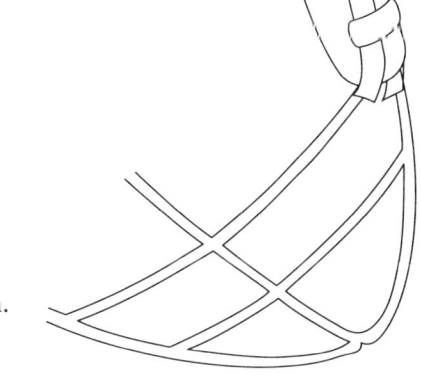

FOOTBALL HERO SANDWICH

1 loaf French bread or 4 small loaves
3 cups cooked chicken, diced
1/2 cup celery, diced
1/2 cup sliced almonds
3/4 to 1 cup sharp cheddar cheese, grated
2 tablespoons lemon juice

1/2 teaspoon salt
2 teaspoons onion, grated
3/4 cup mayonnaise
1 cup water chestnuts, sliced
1 cup mushrooms
1/8 teaspoon curry

PRE-GAME:
Slice loaves down center without going through.
Scoop out some of the bread contents. Discard or make bread crumbs.
Mix remaining ingredients. Stuff into center of loaves.

SECOND QUARTER:
Bake on cookie sheet at 350 degrees for 15 minutes or until hot.
Slice into 2" - 3" pieces.

HALL OF FAME HAM

HALL OF FAME

The Pro Football Hall of Fame is located in Canton, Ohio. Opened in 1963 The Hall now encompasses a four-building 51,000 square-foot facility. The Hall honors the greats of football. It has a 350-seat theater, research library, souvenir shop and other attractions.

The Hall of Fame's 31-member Board of Selectors elects the men to the Hall of Fame. Any fan may also nominate a player by writing to the Hall of Fame. A player is eligible after he's been retired at least five years. Coaches need only be retired-with no time limit requirement. A nominee must receive more than 80 percent approval from the board. Usually 4 to 7 players become new enshrinees each year.

1-5 pound pre-cooked ham or 10-pound uncooked ham.
Whole cloves
White wine
2 medium-sized apples, quartered
1 orange, quartered
2 cinnamon sticks
1 large can crushed pineapple, drained
1/2 to 1 pound brown sugar

PRE-GAME:
Use skinned ham from which excess fat has been removed.
Score ham and stud with cloves.
Place ham in roasting pan. Add half white wine and half water until ham is 1/3 submerged in liquid.
Quarter apples and oranges, unpeeled. Top ham with 1 cup crushed pineapple. Add 2 cinnamon sticks, broken.
Keep adding liquid since baking will evaporate it.

PRE-COOKED HAM

FIRST QUARTER:
Heat pre-cooked ham. Baste every 15 minutes.

SECOND QUARTER:
Top with brown sugar approximately 1/4" thick and baste every 10 minutes.

HALF-TIME:
Remove cloves; slice ham.

UNCOOKED HAM

PRE-GAME:
Bake according to directions for size of ham.
Bake at 300 degrees for 2 hours, basting every 15-20 minutes.

FIRST QUARTER:
Top with brown sugar and bake for 1 hour longer. Baste every 15-20 minutes.

HALF-TIME:
Remove cloves; slice ham.

COUNTDOWN CURRIED FRUIT

1 (29-ounce) can pears
1 (29-ounce) can sliced peaches
1 (17-ounce) can Royal Anne cherries or maraschino cherries
1 (20-ounce) can pineapple
1 (11-ounce) can Mandarin oranges
1 (17-ounce) can apricots, peeled
1/2 cup currants
3/4 cup sugar
1/4 teaspoon salt (optional)
3 tablespoons margarine
3 tablespoons flour
1 (3-ounce) package slivered almonds, toasted
1/2-1 teaspoon curry
1/2 cup white wine

PRE-GAME:
Drain cans of fruit. Save 3/4 cup of the fruit juice to mix with currants, sugar, salt, margarine and flour. Heat but do not boil. Stir mixture.
Add almonds, curry and wine.
Add fruit. Bake at 325 degrees for 30 minutes.

SUPER BOWL RING

1 (16-ounce) can dark cherries
1 (13-ounce) can crushed pineapple
1 (3.4-ounce) package black cherry gelatin
1 (3-ounce) package cream cheese, softened, cut in pieces
1/2 cup pecans, chopped

PRE-GAME:
Drain cherries and save 3/4 cup juice. Drain pineapple and save 1/4 cup juice.
Dissolve gelatin in 1 cup water
Stir in cream cheese pieces and fruit juices.
Add pineapple, cherries and pecans.
Pour into ring mold.

HALF-TIME:
Unmold. Surround with INSTANT REPLAY FRESH FRUIT if there is any left over from brunch.

SUPER BOWL RING

Every professional football player hopes to play in the Super Bowl and be a part of the winning team. Besides the prize money (eg. in 1990 the 49ers garnered $36,000 and Denver received $18,000) to the victors, each winning player is presented with a Super Bowl Ring.

WILD CARD WILD RICE AND SAUSAGE CASSEROLE

1 pound ground round
1 pound sausage—not too hot
1 box wild rice
1/2 box brown rice (or 1/2 pound)
1 cup celery, chopped
1 cup onion, chopped
1-1/2 cups fresh mushrooms, sliced
1 can mushroom soup
1/2 teaspoon sage (optional)

PRE-GAME:
Cook rice separately. Cook sausage and ground round, drain off fat. Saute celery, onion and mushrooms; set aside. Mix all ingredients. Add water if it seems too stiff. Place in a casserole.

FIRST QUARTER:
(5-10 minutes before the end of the *Quarter*.)
Bake at 350 degrees for 45 minutes to 1 hour or until bubbly.

> **WILD CARD**
> Divisional non-champion (second-place divisional teams) from each conference earn a wild card spot in the playoffs.
>
> Through a complicated system wild card teams play each other or the division champion with the third-best record in the first round play-off games.
>
> In the conference championship a wild card team may play host only if facing another wild card team!
>
> This system was designed by an unbalanced football genius who wished to confuse all of us.

MOST VALUABLE PLAYER MOCHA CHIP CHEESECAKE

6 tablespoons margarine, melted
1-1/2 cups chocolate wafer crumbs
2 tablespoons sugar
3 (8-ounce) packages cream cheese
1 cup sugar
4 eggs
1/3 cup whipping cream or milk
1 tablespoon instant coffee
1 teaspoon vanilla
1 (6-ounce) package mini chocolate chips, semi-sweet

PRE-GAME:
CRUST: Butter 10" spring-form pan. Combine margarine, crumbs and sugar. Press into pan. Bake 10 minutes at 350 degrees. Cool.

FILLING: Reduce oven temperature to 200 degrees.
Beat cheese until soft. Add sugar. Beat in eggs one at a time. Stir in cream, coffee and vanilla. Beat 1 minute or more. Pour half the mixture into pan. Fold chips into remaining batter. Carefully pour chip batter into pan. Bake 2 hours at 200 degrees. Cool. Refrigerate.

Yield: 16 servings

"THE PARTY'S OVER" PINA COLADA CAKE

1 box white cake mix—no pudding
1/2 cup water
1/4 cup oil
4 eggs
1/3 cup Rum—light or dark
1 (8-ounce) can crushed pineapple, drained
1 (3.4-ounce) small package French vanilla instant pudding

FROSTING

1 (3.4-ounce) small package French vanilla instant pudding
3 tablespoons rum
1 (8-ounce) can undrained crushed pineapple
1 (8-ounce) carton non-dairy whipped topping
Flaked coconut

PRE-GAME:

CAKE:
Mix all ingredients until well blended; pour into greased and floured 9" x 12" pan; bake at 350 degrees (325 degrees for glass pan) 35-40 minutes. Do not underbake. When cake is completely cooled, frost and refrigerate.

FROSTING:
Mix first 3 ingredients thoroughly and add non-dairy whipped topping. Frost and sprinkle with coconut. Refrigerate.

Whenever a score was considerably lopsided, Don Meredith, then a sportscaster for Monday Night Football, would begin singing "The Party's Over." Meredith enjoyed popularity in the telecast booth with his repartee. Prior to television Meredith starred as a quarterback for the Dallas Cowboys.

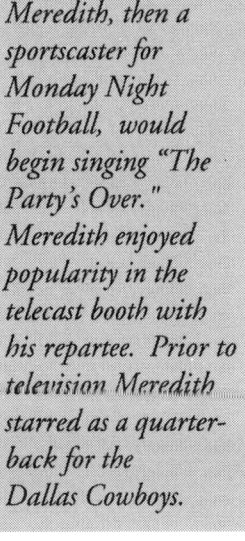

SOUPER BOWL SUNDAE

MENU

Raspbrie Shell

Split Pea Soup   Mushroom Soup

Steak Sandwiches

Sundaes—Chocolate, Strawberry, Vanilla Ice Cream or Frozen Yogurt

Shredded Carrot Sheet Cake

RASPBRIE SHELL

Approach a Souper Bowl Party with food that is easy to eat and serve. Have pots of warm hearty soups on the stove. Set up the buffet table near by. Have bowls and plates ready for guests to serve themselves.

1-2 frozen puff pastry shells
1 (4.5 ounce) package brie cheese

Raspberry preserves
1 large egg
1 tablespoon water

PRE-GAME:
Roll out pastry shells in circles.
Place brie in center of 1 shell. Brush raspberry preserves over brie.
Cover brie with pastry. Place seam-side down on baking sheet. Beat egg and water together. Brush over entire dough.
Bake at 375 degrees 10-15 minutes or until light golden brown.
Serve with pear slices or crackers.

SPLIT PEA SOUP

1 pound package green split peas
1-1/2 quarts water
3 cans chicken broth
2 smoked ham hocks
1-1/3 cups celery, chopped
1 cup onions, chopped
2 cups carrots, shredded or chopped

3 tablespoons margarine
3 tablespoons parsley
1 bay leaf
1/4 teaspoon thyme
Salt and pepper
Sour cream (optional)
Dry sherry (optional)

PRE-GAME:
Wash and sort peas; add water. Bring to boiling; simmer 2 minutes. Remove from heat; cover and let stand 1 or more hours. Add broth, ham hocks, celery and parsley. Boil then reduce heat to simmer 45 minutes, stirring occasionally. Saute onions and carrots in margarine. Add to pot with bay leaf and thyme. Simmer covered, 2 hours or until peas are soft. Remove ham hocks; cut meat off bone, removing any excess fat. Set aside meat.
Place soup through food processor or sieve, if desired. Return meat to soup. Add salt and pepper to taste.

SECOND QUARTER:
Heat soup in oven or atop stove.

HALF-TIME:
Optional: Serve soup with a dollop of sour cream topped with sherry.

Note: The flavor of smoked ham hocks is ideal, but you need to buy meaty ones. If unable to find, use a ham bone.

FRESH CREAM OF MUSHROOM SOUP

1/2 medium onion, sliced	1 cup cream (half and half)
3 cups fresh mushrooms, sliced	2 tablespoons sherry
4 tablespoons margarine	1/2 teaspoon pepper
4 tablespoons flour	1/4 teaspoon nutmeg (optional)
4 cups chicken broth	Salt to taste

PRE-GAME:
Saute onion and mushrooms in margarine approximately 5 minutes. Add flour and blend. Add chicken broth or stock. Cool slightly. Add cream, and sherry and spices.

SECOND QUARTER:
Heat soup.

AUDIBLE
The quarterback lines up over the center. He realizes the play called in the huddle won't work against this defense. Calling a live color and number (eg. red 52) serves notice to his team that he's changing the play.

You can make changes in recipes too when you see an ingredient you don't like . Fresh mushroom soup instead of canned. Parsley instead of cilantro. Fresh herbs instead of dried herbs in a 4-3:1 ratio.

STEAK SANDWICHES

2 pounds flank steak
2 tablespoons margarine
4 cups onions, sliced

1 cup sour cream
1/2 teaspoons prepared horseradish
12 slices French bread

MARINADE
Use marinade recipe for *Roughing the Kicker Kabobs* p. 98.

PRE-GAME:
Prick steak with fork.
Marinate steak one hour or more.

SECOND QUARTER:
Saute onions in margarine. Set aside.
SAUCE: Mix sour cream and horseradish.
Broil steak 3" from heat. 5-7 minutes.

HALF-TIME:
Serve onions, horseradish sauce, meat and bread slices.
Have fans assemble their own sandwiches.

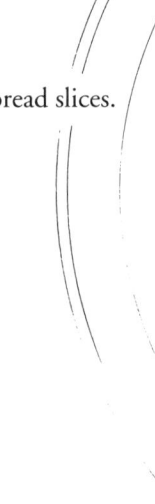

SUNDAES

Set out a sundae bar. Fans can scoop up their own concoctions.

Ice cream or frozen yogurt: Chocolate, vanilla and strawberry
Sauces: Hot fudge, strawberry and pineapple
Toppings: Whipped cream, nuts, cherries, bananas, mini-chocolate chips and crushed oreo cookies.

SHREDDED CARROT CAKE

2 cups flour
1-1/2 teaspoons baking soda
2 teaspoons baking powder
1 teaspoon salt
2-3 teaspoons cinnamon
1-1/2 cups oil
2 cups sugar

4 eggs
2 cups carrots, shredded
1 (8-ounce) can crushed pineapple, drained
1 cup walnuts, chopped

BRANDY CHEESE FROSTING

1 (3-ounce) package cream cheese
1/2 pound powdered sugar
1 ounce brandy

1-1/2 tablespoons light cream
1/4 teaspoon vanilla

PRE-GAME:
Combine dry ingredients. Add oil, sugar and egg.
Mix. Add carrots, pineapple and nuts.
Bake at 350 degrees 40-45 minutes in 9" x 13" pan.

FROSTING: Whip cream cheese. Add remaining ingredients.
Add more sugar as needed for spreading consistency.
Add green food color to frosting. Decorate with white frosting to simulate football field markers. Make goal posts using plastic straws.

DRESSING ROOM

BASIL DRESSING

2 cups fresh basil leaves
2 large garlic cloves
1/2 cup Parmesan cheese
2 tablespoons Romano cheese
1/4 cup pine nuts
1/2 cup olive oil
Salt and pepper to taste

PRE-GAME:
Combine basil, garlic, cheese, and nuts in a food processor. Slowly add olive oil. Blend well. Season with salt and pepper

> **LOCKER ROOM**
> *Away from the stadium lights, the roar of the crowd and the "Hi Mom" television faces dwell some of the games unsung heroes. This is the domain of the equipment managers, trainers, strength and conditioning coordinators and their assistants.*

FRENCH DRESSING

1 cup oil
2/3 cup sugar
2/3 cup ketchup or chili sauce
1/2 cup vinegar
2 teaspoons paprika
1 teaspoon salt
1 large clove garlic, minced
1 large onion, grated

PRE-GAME:
Blend all ingredients. Chill. Shake vigorously before using.

POPPY SEED DRESSING

1-1/2 cups sugar
2 teaspoons dry mustard
2 teaspoons salt
2/3 cup vinegar
3 tablespoons onion juice
2 cups salad oil (never olive oil)
3 tablespoons poppy seed

PRE-GAME:
Mix sugar, dry mustard, salt and vinegar.
Add onion juice and salad oil; blend well.
Add poppy seeds and stir again.

BLUE CHEESE DRESSING

1 pint mayonnaise
1/2 cup buttermilk
1/2 teaspoon dry mustard
1/2 teaspoon Worcestershire sauce
Dash pepper
2-1/2 to 3-1/2 ounces Roquefort or blue cheese

PRE-GAME:
Blend all ingredients saving 1/2 the cheese. When mixture is fully blended, add remaining chunks of cheese.
Store in refrigerator in a jar.

THOUSAND ISLAND DRESSING

2 ounces pimiento, chopped
2 ounces green olives, sliced
1/4 cup bell pepper, chopped
1/2 cup onion, chopped
1/2 cup ketchup
2 cups mayonnaise

PRE-GAME:
Mix ingredients. (You may wish to add more pimiento.)
Store dressing in refrigerator.

Yield: 1 quart

WALNUT DRESSING

1/3 cup walnut oil
2 tablespoons white wine vinegar
1/2 teaspoon salt
Freshly grround white peppercorns
1/4 cup walnuts, chopped

PRE-GAME:
Whisk oil and vinegar. Add salt and pepper. Add walnuts. Place in jar. Refrigerate.

Yield: 1/2 cup

ROOKIE RECIPE TIPS

You have probably done some cooking or baking in the past.
Here are some helpful tips not only for rookie cooks, but also seasoned veterans.

BASIC MEASUREMENTS

Pinch = less than 1/8 teaspoon

Dash = 3 drops to less than 1/4 teaspoon

3 teaspoons = 1 tablespoon

2 tablespoons = 1 ounce

4 tablespoons = 1/4 cup

5-1/3 tablespoons = 1/3 cup

12 tablespoons = 3/4 cup

1 cup = 8 ounces = 1/2 pint

2 cups = 1 pint

2 pints = 1 quart

4 quarts = 1 gallon

1 quart = about 1 litre (10% less)

CAN SIZES

6-ounce can = 3/4 cup

8-ounce can = 1 cup, serves 2

No. 1 can = 11 ounces = 1-1/4 cups, serves 3

No. 303 can = 16 ounces = 2 cups, serves 4

No. 2 can = 20 ounces = 2-1/2 cups, serves 6

No. 2-1/2 can = 28 ounces = 3-1/2 cups, serves 7-8

No. 3 can = 5-3/4 cups, serves 10-12

TEMPERATURES

32 degrees F = Water Freezes

68-74 degrees F = Room Temperature

205 degrees F = Water Simmers

212 degrees F = Water Boils

350 degrees F = Baking

400 degrees F = Hot Oven

450 degrees F = Very Hot Oven

500 degrees F = Broiling

To convert Fahrenheit to Celsius—subtract 32 from
the Fahrenheit scale, multiply by 5, divide by 9 = Celsius.

FOOD EQUIVALENTS:

Apples—1 pound = 3 medium or 3 cups sliced

Avocados—1 medium = 2 cups, cubed

Beef, cooked—1 pound = 3 cups, shredded

Bread crumbs, dry—1 slice = 1/3 cup

Butter or margarine—1 stick = 1/4 pound = 1/2 cup

Cabbage—1 pound = 4 cups, shredded

Carrots—1 pound = 7-8 medium = 4 cups, diced

Cheese—
    Cheddar—1 pound = 4-5 cups grated
    Cottage—1/2 pound = 1 cup

Chicken—3-1/2 pounds, raw = 2 cups, cooked, diced

Chocolate—unsweetened, semi-sweet or sweetened— 1 square = 1 ounce

Cream, heavy—1 cup = 2 cups, whipped

Flour (All-Purpose)—1 pound = 4 cups sifted

Garlic Powder—1/8 teaspoon powder = 1 small clove

Gelatin (unflavored)—envelope contains 1 tablespoon; will gel 2 cups liquid

Graham Crackers—12 squares = 1 cup fine crumbs

Herbs—1: 3 or 4 ratio; e.g. 1 teaspoon dry = 3-4 teaspoons fresh

Lemon—Juice of 1 lemon = 2 to 3 tablespoons
        Rind of 1 lemon, grated = 2 teaspoons

Mushrooms, fresh—1 pound = 36 medium = 5 cups, sliced

Nuts—(Shelled)
    Pecans—1 pound = 4 cups nutmeats

A rookie is a player in his first year of participation in a major professional sport. Rookies already know a great deal about football from their college days, but pro ball is a new level of play. Many rookies are moved from the position they played in college to a new position.

　　　　　Walnuts—1 pound = 4 cups nutmeats
　　　　　Peanuts—1 pound = 3 cups nutmeats

Orange—Juice of 1 orange = 1/3 to 1/2 cup
　　　　Rind of 1 orange = 2 to 3 tablespoons

Potatoes, white—1 pound = 4 medium = 2-1/2 cups, diced and cooked

Sugar
　　Granulated—1 pound = 2 cups
　　Brown—1 pound = 2-1/4 cups, firmly packed
　　Confectioner's (powdered)—1 pound = 3-1/2 cups, sifted

Tomatoes—1-1/3 cups fresh tomatoes simmered = 1 cup canned tomatoes

WINNERS

Winning is a team effort, not unlike assembling this cookbook. My thanks and appreciation to so many for their assistance.

My family and friends—Mary Albert, Bobbie Barnett, Marlene Barnett, Barbara Baugh, Judy Berg, Susan Brown, Lynn Brandon, Marie Demler, Jean Grover, Roy Huhndorf, Lynn King, Ginny Landry, Norma Lang, Susan Lounsberry, Lynn Lucurell, Linda McCloud, Kathy Moore, Helen Moore, Ida Middlesworth, Bonnie Nygren, Ann Parrish, Cathy and Ed Rasmuson, Margaret Pugh, Ashley and Denise Reed, Cookie Roemer, John Rogers, Mary Ann Swalling, Marge and George Valley, Pat Walsh, Carol Walton, Phil Zarro, Marguerite and Bob Zwissler—for all their great recipes.

To Ray Ashton, Travis Cantrell, Jan Carter, Scott Galey, Bete Gillespie, Bill Green, Bob Juliano, Marthy Johnson, Steve Kruschwitz, Larry Lloyd, John McKay, James Nagaoka and Celia Nibeck for technical assistance.

To Art & International Productions—Sasha Sagan and Jim Tilly—who make assembling a book fun.

To Dr. Jane Evanson, Alaska Pacific University, for her knowledge, support and nudging to complete this book.

To two winners in my life, Bill and Tyler for their help in completing this project.

FUMBLE-FREE GRID

ENTER DRAWN NUMBERS

TEAM "A" _____

Example of drawn numbers:
5 3 8 0 9 7 6 2 4 1

TEAM "B"
9
4
3
8
0
7
6
2
5
1

| 1 | 2 | 3 | 4 | 5 | 6 | 7 | 8 | 9 | 0 |

These numbers can be copied and used for drawing.

196

GUESS THE SCORE

There are many ways to play or bet on the score. This is perhaps one of the more popular.

1. Duplicate the grid (on the opposite page) on an 8-1/2" x 11" sheet of paper.

2. As each person/couple arrives, the home team should designate the maximum number of spaces each person is allowed and the price per space.

    There are 100 spaces available. If you have 10 or more people you may wish to bet up to $1.00 or more per space. When you have fewer people in attendance you may wish to bet less. Prior to the end of the first quarter you should try to have all squares filled.

3. List one team's names under "Team A" and the other on the "Team B" line.

4. Tear up 10 small pieces of paper which have been numbered 0-9. Place pieces in a basket and have a fan draw and call out each number. Another fan should fill in the horizontal spaces under the team "A" line.

5. Repeat for Team "B" and fill out vertical spaces.

6. If 10 people have selected 10 spaces for $1.00 each
    **the first, second and third quarters are worth $20.00 each.
    The fourth quarter score winner receives $40.00.** You may wish to try other variations.

7. If the first quarter score is:
    Team "A"   —   10
    Team "B"   —   7

    The last digit, 0-7, determines the winner.

BIBLIOGRAPHY

Dobler, Conrad and Vic Carucci. They Call Me Dirty. New York: Jove Books, 1988.

Hollander, Zander, ed. The Complete Handbook of Pro Football. New York: Signet, 1990.

Horrigan, Joe. The Official Pro Football Hall of Fame Answer Book. New York: Simon & Schuster, 1990.

Madden, John and Dave Anderson. One Knee Equals Two Feet: and Everything Else You Need to Know About Football. New York: Jove Books, 1986.

National Football League. Official 1990 National Football League Record and Fact Book. New York: Workman Publishing Co., 1990.

Riffenburgh, Beau and David Boss. Running Wild: A Photographic Tribute to the NFL's Greateat Runners. New York: New American Library, 1987.

Riggins, John and Jack Winter. Gameplan: The Language & Strategy of Pro Football. Santa Barbara: Santa Barbara Press, 1984.

Smith, Don R. The Official Pro Football Hall of Fame Book of Superstars. New York: Simon & Shuster, 1990.

Sullivan, George, ed. Football Rules Illustrated. New York: Simon & Schuster, 1981.

TEAM NAMES AND COLORS

AFC
American Football Conference

Atlanta Falcons
    Red, black, white and silver

Chicago Bears
    Navy blue, orange and white

Dallas Cowboys
    Royal blue, metallic silver blue and white

Detroit Lions
    Honolulu blue and silver

Green Bay Packers
    Dark green, gold and white

Los Angeles Rams
    Royal blue, gold and white

Minnesota Vikings
    Purple, gold and white

New Orleans Saints
    Old gold, black and white

New York Giants
    Blue, red and white

Philadelphia Eagles
    Kelly green, silver and white

Phoenix Cardinals
    Cardinal red, black and white

San Francisco 49ers
    Forty Niners gold and scarlet

Tampa Bay Buccaneers
    Florida orange, white and red

Washington Redskins
    Burgundy and gold

NFC
National Football Conference

Buffalo Bills
    Royal blue, scarlet and white

Cincinnati Bengals
    Black, orange and white

Cleveland Browns
    Seal Brown, orange and white

Denver Broncos
    Orange, royal blue and white

Houston Oilers
    Columbia Blue, scarlet and white

Indianapolis Colts
    Royal blue and white

Kansas City Chiefs
    Red, gold and white

Los Angeles Raiders
    Silver and black

Miami Dolphins
    Aqua, coral and white

New England Patriots
    Red, white and blue

New York Jets
    Kelly green and white

Pittsburgh Steelers
    Black and gold

San Diego Chargers
    Navy blue, white and gold

Seattle Seahawks
    Blue, green and silver

FOOTBALL INDEX

There are so many other players, records and memorable plays that I wish I could have included. If I've left out your favorite football personality or term, see page 207.

PERSONALITIES

Troy Aikman, 139
George Allen, 157
Marcus Allen, 150
Lance Alworth, 140
Alan Ameche, 150
Raymond Berry, 144
Fred Biletnikoff, 140
George Blanda, 125, 138
Brian Bosworth, 137
Terry Bradshaw, 29, 140
John Brodie, 140
Jim Brown, 133
Paul Brown, 157
Dick Butkus, 134
Earl Campbell, 150
Billy Cannon, 150
Gino Cappelletti, 125
Howard Cosell, 158
Randall Cunningham, 139
Larry Czonka, 151
Lenny Dawson, 140
Tom Dempsey, 153
Dan Dierdorf, 135
Tony Dorsett, 150
John Elway, 146
Tom Flores, 157
Fearsome Foursome, 145
Dan Fouts, 29
Walt Garrison, 150
Joe Gibbs, 157
Frank Gifford, 142, 158
Bud Grant, 157
Joe Green, 131
Roosevelt Grier, 145

Bob Griese, 140
Lou Groza, 125
George Halas, 126
Franco Harris, 150
Bob Hayes, 29
Calvin Hill, 150
Bo Jackson, 137
Ron Jaworski, 128
John Henry Johnson, 147
Deacon Jones, 145
Ed "Too Tall" Jones, 135
Sonny Jurgenson, 140
Jim Kiick, 150
Kenny King, 152
Chuck Knox, 157
Tom Landry, 157
Steve Largent, 124
Bobby Layne, 140
Bob Lilly, 135
Vince Lombardi, 157
Howie Long, 135
Ronnie Lott, 132
Lamar Lundy, 145
John Madden, 157, 158
Errol Mann, 153
Archie Manning, 136
Lawrence McCutcheon, 150
Hugh McElhenny, 147, 149
Don Meredith, 29, 150, 185
Million Dollar Backfield, 147
Memorable Linemen and
    Defensive Backs, 135
Joe Montana, 29, 141
Mercury Morris, 29
Mark Moseley, 125
Mr. Inside, 29
Mr. Outside, 29
Chuck Muncie, 29
Steve Myhra, 144

Joe Namath, 127
Chuck Noll, 157
Merlin Olsen, 145
Orange Crush, 146
Walter Payton, 129
Drew Pearson, 29
Joe Perry, 147
Jim Plunkett, 152
Mike Quick, 128
Jerry Rice, 141
John Riggins, 148
Barry Sanders, 139
Gayle Sayers, 150
Secretary of Defense, 145
Don Shula, 157
O.J. Simpson, 128
Snake, The, 152
Special Teams, 156
Ken Stabler, 152
Bart Starr, 140
Roger Staubach, 29, 140
Jan Stenerud, 125
Lynn Swann, 29, 140
Fran Tarkenton, 143
Lawrence Taylor, 135
Y. A. Tittle, 147
Jim Turner, 125
Johnny Unitas, 123, 130
Jeff Van Note, 135
Paul Warfield, 140
Danny White, 140

200

STADIUMS 49, 52-75

TERMS - RULES - PENALTIES

All-American Football Conference, 48
American Football Conference, 48, 199
American Football League, 48
AstroTurf, brief history, 50
Audible, 187
Automatic First Down, 117
Ball, 16
Basic T Formation, 34
Blitz, 45, 170
Block, 108
Boxman, 161
Chain Crew, 30, 161
    Boxman and Rodmen, 161
Clipping, 115
Coin Toss, 22
Conversion, 44
Defense, 77, 78, 93-105
Defensive Formation, 94
Defensive Line, 93
    Cornerback, 102, 103
    End, 95, 98
    Linebacker, 99-101
    Linemen, 95-98
    Tackle, 96-97
    Safety, 104-105
Downs, 30
Draft, 164
Fair Catch, 118
Fake, The, 33
Fans, 10, 13, 162, 163
Field Goal, 36
Field Support, 155-163
First and Ten, 41
Flanker, 81
Forward Pass Rules, 112
Free-Agent, 164
Free Kick, 111
Hall of Fame, 182
Handoff, 111
Home Team, 11
Instant Replay, 177
Intentional Grounding, 47
Jersey Numbering System, 28
Lateral Pass, 113
Most Valuable Player, 184

Nasty, 31
National Football Conference, 48, 199
National Football League, 48, 199
Nickel Defense, 33
Offense, 76, 78-91
Offensive Line, 29
    Center 79, 84
    Fullback, 79, 89
    Guard, 79, 83, 85
    Halfback, 79, 90
    Quarterback, 79, 91
    Running Backs, 79, 89, 90
    Tackle, 79, 82, 86
    Tight End, 79, 87
    Wide Receiver, 79, 88
Offensive Players, 80
Officials, 156
Off-Setting Penalties, 109
Offside, 119
Onside Kick, 114
Party's Over, 185
Pass Interference, 120
Personal Foul, 116
Playing Field, 18, 76-77
Pink Dog, 172
Point-After, 36
Pre-Season, 56
Press Box, 159
Pro Bowl, 178
Red Dog, 172
Referees, 156
Rookies, 193
Roughing the Kicker, 98
Sack the Quarterback, 145
Safety (score), 36
Score, 36
Scrimmage, Line of, 21
Snap, 24
Spearing, 38
Substitution, 154
Sudden Death, 9, 12, 123, 128, 130
Super Bowl, 173-183
Super Bowl Ring, 183
Taxi-Squad, 27
Touchdown, 36, 121
Turnover, 25
T.V. Crew, 159
Wide Receiver, 79, 88
Wild Card, 184

RECIPE INDEX

Appetizers, The Kickoff, 13-47
   Artichoke Nibbles, 21
   Avocado Crab Dip, 32
   Black-Eyed Pea Dip, 32
   Caviar Mousse, 22
   Caviar Sour Cream Spread, 23
   Cheese Puffs, 37
   Clam Spread, 42
   Crab Dip in Sheepherder Bread, 39
   Crab Mold, 39
   Crab-Stuffed Cheese Puffs, 37
   Chili Con Queso, 34
   Dill Dip, Basic, 34
   Dressed Shrimp, 40
   Eggplant Appetizer, 19
   Pate, Fake, 33
   Gravlax, 42
   Guacamole Dunk, 27
   Honey Dip, 44
   Hot Crab Dip, 31
   Layered Mexican Dip, 26
   Mexicali Sombrero Skins, 29
   Mushrooms, marinated, 20
   Mushrooms, stuffed, 20
   Mussels, First and Ten, 41
   Nachos, On the Numbers, 28
   Nasturtium Dip, 31
   Nickel Defense Dip, 33
   Olive Cheese Ball, 17
   Oyster Fritters, 36
   Parmesan Cheese Ball, 17
   Party Meatballs, Blitzing, 45
   Peanutty Dip, 34
   Peppered Cheese Ball, 16
   Pickled Salmon, 38
   Pimiento Dip, 30
   Potato Pancakes Caviar, 23
   Quesadillas, Hearty, 28
   Raspbrie Shell, 186
   Reuben Dip, 30
   Salmon Ball, 15
   Sesame Chicken, Honey Dip, 44
   Smoked Salmon, 43
   Snacks, 176
   Spinach, Scrimmage, 26
   Steak Tartare, 47
   Teriyaki Chicken Wings, 20-Yard Line, 46
   Tex Mex Beef Dip, 25
   Tortilla Pie, Taxi Squad, 27
   Tortilla Turnovers, 25
   Undressed Shrimp, 40
   Vegetable Squares, 18
   Whole Wheat Pita Crisps, 19

Basics, 194-196
   Measurements, 194
   Food Equivalents, 195-196

Breads, 107-121
   Automatic Honey-Sesame Bread
     (Automatic First Down), 117
   Bacon Cheese Bread (Throw a Block), 108
   Bread Sticks (Onside Kick), 114
   Carmel Pull-Apart Breakfast Rolls, 179
   Corn Bread Squares (Clipping), 115
   Cottage Cheese Beer Bread (Fair Catch), 118
   Croutons (T.V. Crew), 158
   Foccacia Bread (Forward Pass), 112
   Onion Cake (Offsides), 119
   Gourmet French Bread (Personal Foul), 116
   Grapefruit Nut Bread, 179
   Hawaiian Bread (Pro Bowl), 178
   Healthy Muffins, 180
   Herb Bread (Handoff), 111
   Herb-Buttered French Bread (Free-Kick), 111
   Mozzarella Loaf (Lateral Pass), 113
   Onion, Cheese and Chile Bread
     (Unsportsmanlike), 110
   Onion Herb Bread
     (Off-Setting Penalties), 109
   Pepper, Parmesan, Paprika Twists
     (Pass Interference), 120
   Rolls, Touchdown, 121
   Whole Wheat Pita Crisps, 19

Casseroles
- Brunch Casserole, Superstar, 180
- Curried Fruit, Countdown, 183
- Fractured Turkey Tacos, 86
- Tamale Pie, 96
- Tuna Noodle Casserole, 170

Cheese
- Bacon Cheese Bread, 108
- Baked Fish au Gratin, 83
- Cheese Chowder, 84
- Cheese Puffs, 37
- Chili Con Queso, 24
- Cottage Cheese Beer Bread, 118
- Feta, Olives and Pine Nut Salad, 53
- Gruyere, Walnut Salad and Vinaigrette, 59
- Monterey Jack Melange Salad, 68
- Mozzarella Loaf, 113
- Mozzarella-Mushroom Salad, 66
- Olive Cheese Ball, 17
- Parmesan Cheese Ball, 17
- Pepper, Parmesan, Paprika Strips, 120
- Peppered Cheese Ball, 16
- Raspbrie Shell, 186
- Romano, Romaine, Red Leaf Salad, 57

Children's Food—Fussy Fans, 170-172
- Beef and Beans Casserole, 172
- Corn Dogs, 172
- Party's Pizzas, 171
- Spaghetti, 171
- Tuna Noodle Casserole, 170

Desserts
Cakes
- Apple-Praline Cake, (Archie Manning), 136
- Apricot Chocolate Bombe, (Quarterbacks), 140
- B and B Multi-Million Dollar Cake, (Bosworth and Bo), 137
- Bananas Foster Torte, (Fran Tarkenton), 143
- Berry and Citrus Torte, (Raymond Berry), 144
- Everybody's Favorite Cookie Sheet Cake, (Joe Montana), 141
- Memorable Chocolate Mousse Cake, (Linemen and Defensive Backs), 135
- Mocha Chip Cheesecake, (Most Valuable Player), 184
- Pina Colada Cake, "The Party's Over," 185
- Snowball Cake, 140

Cookies, Brownies and Bars
- A Lot of Lemon Bars, (Ronnie Lott), 132
- Charter Caramel Cookies, 129
- Chocolate Chip Bars, (Joe Namath), 127
- Chocolate Pepper Cookies, (Kickers), 125
- Double Chocolate Crumble Crisp Bars, (George Halas), 126
- Everybody's Favorite Cookie Sheet Cake, (Joe Montana), 141
- German Chocolate and Cream Cheese Brownies, (Jim Brown), 133
- Gingersnap Bars, (Johnny Unitas), 130
- M-M-M-Monster Cookies, (Joe Green), 131
- Orange Jewel Cookies, (O. J. Simpson), 128
- Pecan Chocolate Chip Cookies, (Steve Largent), 124
- Peanut Butter Cookies, (Walter Payton), 129
- Quick Cookies, (Jaworski to Quick), 128
- Rocky Road Brownies, (Dick Butkus), 134
- Shredded Carrot Cake, 189

Miscellaneous
- Ambrosia Cream, 137
- Brandy Cheese Frosting, 188
- Fearsome Foursome Four Layered Pistachio Dessert, 145
- Rocky Road Frosting, 134
- Sundaes, 188

Mousse
- Memorable Chocolate Mousse Cake, Linemen and Defensive Backs, 135

Pies
- Banana Split the Uprights Pizza Pie Dessert (Tom Dempsey), 153
- Best Ever Pecan Pie (Frank Gifford), 142
- Brandy Alexander Pie (John Riggins), 148
- Key Lime (Larry Czonka), 151
- King Coconut Custard Pie (Hugh McElhenney), 149
- Million Dollar Backfield Shredded Apple Pie, 147

Desserts, *continued*
　Pie Crusts—Food Processor and
　　Traditional, 195
　Souffle
　　Cold Orange Crush Souffle,
　　(John Elway), 146

Entrees—Offense and Defense
　Baked White Fish, au Gratin (Guard), 83
　Basil Burgers (Linebacker), 99
　Beef Bourguignon (Defensive Back), 103-104
　Beef Enchiladas (Defensive End), 95
　Beef Fajitas and Salsa
　　(Sack the Quarterback), 100
　Beef or Lamb Kabobs
　　(Roughing the Kicker), 98
　Beef Stroganoff (Defensive Formation), 94
　Cheese and Seafood Chowder (Center), 84
　Chicken Enchiladas (Tight End), 87
　Chicken Florentine (Fullback), 89
　Chicken, Grilled or Barbecued
　　(Quarterback), 91
　Chili (Cornerback), 102
　Fractured Turkey Tacos (Tackle), 86
　Halibut (Halfback), 90
　Lasagna (Defensive Linemen), 97
　Meatloaf, Seasoned (Free-Safety), 105
　Onion Soup (Offensive Players), 80
　Pita Sandwiches (Guard the Pocket), 85
　Roast Beef Pasta (Rushing the Passer), 101
　Swordfish Shish Kabob and Aloha Salsa
　　(Flanker), 81
　Tamale Pie (Defensive Tackle), 96
　Teriyaki Salmon (Tackle), 82
　Vegetable Soup, Savory (Safety), 102
　Wild Rice and Chicken Vol-au-Vent
　　(Wide Receivers), 88

Fruits
　A Lot of Lemon Bars, 132
　Apple-Praline Cake, 136
　Avocado Citrus Salad, 52

　Banana Split the Uprights
　　Pizza Pie Dessert, 153
　Bananas Foster Torte, 143
　Berry and Citrus Torte, 144
　Cold Orange Crush Souffle, 146
　Curried Fruit, 183
　Fresh Fruit, 177, 183
　Grapefruit Nut Bread, 179
　24-Hour Cherry Salad, 63
　Key Lime Pie, 151
　King Coconut Custard Pie, 149
　Peanutty Dip with Fruit, 34

Grains—Rice and Beans
　Baked Beans, 159
　Beef and Beans Casserole, 172
　Grits, 160
　Rice, Referee's, 156
　Spicy Rice, 156
　Wild Rice and Sausage Casserole, 184

Herbs
　Dill Dip, Basic, with Vegetables, 34
　Herb Bread, 111
　Herb-Buttered French Bread, 111
　Pepper, Parmesan, Paprika Twists, 120

Meats
　Beef
　　Basil Burgers, 99
　　Beef and Beans Casserole, 172
　　Beef Bourguignon, 103-104
　　Beef Fajitas and Salsa, 100
　　Beef Kabobs, 98
　　Beef Stroganoff, 94
　　Beefy Enchiladas, 95
　　Chili, 102
　　Corn Dogs, 172
　　Lasagna, 97
　　Meatloaf, 105
　　Party Meat Balls, 45
　　Roast Beef Pasta, 101
　　Savory Vegetable Soup, 102
　　Spaghetti, 171
　　Steak Sandwiches, 188
　　Steak Tartare, 47
　　Tamale Pie, 96
　　Tex Mex Beef Dip, 25

Meat, *continued*
  Corned Beef
      Reuben Dip, 30
  Ham, 182
  Liverwurst
      Pate, 33
  Sausage
      Brunch Casserole, 180
      Pasta/Sausage Salad, 69

Miscellaneous
  Tangy Mustard, 181

Nuts
  Beer Nuts, 175, 176
  Feta, Olives and Pine Nut Salad, 53
  Football Nuts and Bolts, 175, 176
  Gruyere, Walnut Salad, 59
  Peas and Cashew Crunch Salad, 71

Pasta
  Lasagna, 97
  Pasta/Sausage Salad, 69
  Roast Beef Pasta, 101
  Spaghetti, 171
  Tuna Noodle Casserole, 170

Poultry
  Chicken
      Chicken Enchiladas, 87
      Chicken Florentine, 89
      Chinese Chicken and Cilantro Salad, 61
      Chicken Vol-Au-Vent and Wild Rice, 88
      Football Hero Sandwich, 181
      Grilled or Barbecued Chicken, 91
      Sesame Chicken - Honey Dip, 44
      Teriyaki Chicken Wings, 46
  Turkey
      Fractured Turkey Tacos, 86

Salads
  Dressings
      Avocado Dressing, 75
      Basil Dressing, 190
      Blue Cheese Dressing, 73, 191
      Caesar Dressing, 56, 65
      Cobb Dressing, 72
      French Dressing, 190
      Honey-Seed Dressing, 52
      Poppy Seed Dressing, 190
      Red Dressing, 74
      Thousand Island Dressing, 191
      Vermouth Dressing, 67
      Vinaigrette Dressing, 59
      Walnut Dressing, 191
  Greens
      Avocado-Citrus Salad
         (Anaheim Stadium), 52
      Caesar Salad (Superdome), 56
      Chinese Chicken and Cilantro Salad
         (H. H. H. Metrodome), 61
      Cobb Salad (RFK Stadium), 72
      Feta, Olives and Pine nut Salad
         (Atlanta-Fulton County Stadium), 53
      Gruyere and Walnut Salad Vinaigrette
         (Veterans Stadium), 59
      Monterey Jack Melange
         (Jack Murphy Stadium), 68
      Red Tip Salad with Vermouth Dressing
         (Rich Stadium), 67
      Romaine Salad with Blue Cheese Dressing
         (Riverfront Stadium), 73
      Romano, Romaine, Red Leaf Salad
         (Joe Robbie Stadium), 57
      Special Spinach Salad
         (Sun Devil Stadium), 66
      Tex Mex Caesar Salad
         (Texas Stadium), 65
      "Three R" Romaine-Raisin and Red
         Dressing (Three Rivers Stadium), 74
      Tomato, Shrimp, Avocado Salad
         (Tampa Bay Stadium), 75
      Two-Team Meadowlands Garden State
         Salad (Giants Stadium), 60
  Molded
      Aspic Salad (Arrowhead Stadium), 55
      24-Hour Cherry Salad (Hoosier Dome), 63
      Ring Salad (Super Bowl Ring), 183
  Pasta
      Antipasta Salad (Astrodome), 53
      Pasta/Sausage Salad, Pontiac
         (Silverdome), 69
      Peppers and Pickle Pasta Salad
         (Candlestick Park), 62
  Vegetable
      Cabbage Crunch Salad
         (Cleveland Stadium), 63

Vegetable Salads, *continued*
   Cauliflower/Broccoli Salad
     (Foxboro Stadium), 55
   Coliseum Coleslaw
     (Memorial Coliseum), 58
   Peas and Cashews Crunch Salad
     (Kingdome), 70
   Sour Cream Potato Salad (Soldier Field), 71
   Vegetable Layered Salad (Lambeau Field
     and Milwaukee County Stadium), 64

Salsa
  Aloha Salsa, 81
  Mild Fans Salsa, 162
  Salsa with Beef Fajitas, 100
  Wild Fans Salsa, 163

Seafood
  Caviar
    Caviar Sour Cream Spread, 24
    Caviar Mousse, 23
    Potato Pancakes Caviar, 24
  Chowder
    Cheese and Seafood Chowder, 84
  Clams
    Clam Spread, 42
  Crab
    Avocado Crab Dip, 32
    Crab Dip in Sheepherder Bread, 39
    Crab Mold, 39
    Crab-Stuffed Cheese Puffs, 37
  Halibut,
    Halibut and variation, 90
  Oysters
    Oyster Fritters, 36
  Salmon
    Ball, 17
    Gravlax, 42
    Pickled Salmon, 38
    Smoked Salmon, 43
    Teriyaki Salmon, 82

  Shrimp
    Dressed Shrimp, 40
    Tomato, Shrimp and Avocado Salad, 75
    Undressed Shrimp, 40
  Swordfish
    Shish Kabob, 81
  Tuna
    Noodle Casserole, 170
  White Fish (sole, red snapper, perch)
    Baked Fish au Gratin, 83
Soup
  Cheese and Seafood Chowder, 84
  Mushroom
  Onion Soup, 80
  Savory Vegetable Soup, 102
  Split Pea, 186

Special Support Dishes, 155-163

Super Bowl Fare, 173-189

Vegetables
  Artichoke Nibbles, 21
  Black-Eyed Pea Dip, 32
  Cabbage Crunch Salad, 63
  Cauliflower/Broccoli Salad, 55
  Chinese Chicken and Cilantro Salad, 61
  Eggplant Appetizer, 19
  Mushrooms, 20
    fresh mushroom soup, 187
    marinated, 20
    Mozzarella-Mushroom Salad, 66
    stuffed, 20
  Onions
    Onion Cake, 119
  Peas
    Peas and Cashew Crunch Salad, 71
  Peppers and Pickle Pasta Salad, 62
  Potatoes
    Potato Bar, 15
    Potatoes Gorgonzola, 157
    Mexicali Sombrero Skins, 29
    Potato Pancakes Caviar, 23
    Sour Cream Potato Salad, 71
  Spinach
    Spinach Dip, 21
    Special Spinach Salad, 66
  Vegetable Layered Salad, 64
  Vegetable Squares, 18
  Zucchini/Crust Casserole, 161

If you wish to order additional copies of
FUMBLE FREE: A FOOTBALL COOKBOOK
contact:

Eagle Shore Press

P.O. Box 92477

Anchorage, Alaska 99509-2477

Tel: (907) 277-8422

FAX: (907) 272-4800

Do you have a favorite recipe
for football viewing that you would like to share?
Maybe you'd like to see your favorite football personality
or fact in our next book,
THE FOOTBALL FANS COOKBOOK.
If so, please include the following
1. Name, mailing address and telephone number
2. Source for recipe or fact
(e.g. Recipe belonged to my grandmother;
Fact from <u>World Almanac</u>, 1990, page 100.)

If your contribution is selected,
your name will be acknowledged in the book.
I'm sorry we cannot accept previously copyrighted recipes.

Please send recipes to:
THE FOOTBALL FANS COOKBOOK
P.O. Box 92477
Anchorage, Alaska 99509-2477